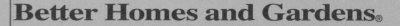

⟪ W9-BJB-290

halloween
Pumpkins &
Parties

101
SPOOKTACULAR
IDEAS

PORTER COUNTY PUBLIC LIBRARY SYSTEM

South Haven Public Library
403 West 700 North
Valparaiso, IN 46383

745.5941 HAL   SH
Halloween pumpkins &
parties : 101 spooktacular
33410006864898

SEP 1 5 2002

Better Homes and Gardens® Books
Des Moines, Iowa

Better Homes and Gardens® Books
An imprint of Meredith® Books

Halloween Pumpkins & Parties
101 Spooktacular Ideas

Editor: Carol Field Dahlstrom
Contributing Editor: Susan M. Banker
Graphic Designer: Angela Haupert Hoogensen
Copy Chief: Terri Fredrickson
Copy and Production Editor: Victoria Forlini
Editorial Operations Manager: Karen Schirm
Managers, Book Production: Pam Kvitne, Marjorie J. Schenkelberg
Contributing Copy Editor: Arianna McKinney
Contributing Proofreaders: Karen Grossman, Colleen Johnson, Karen Schmidt
Photographers: Andy Lyons Cameraworks, Peter Krumhardt, Scott Little
Technical Illustrator: Chris Neubauer Graphics, Inc.
Electronic Production Coordinator: Paula Forest
Editorial and Design Assistants: Kaye Chabot, Mary Lee Gavin, Karen McFadden

Meredith® Books
Editor in Chief: James D. Blume
Design Director: Matt Strelecki
Managing Editor: Gregory H. Kayko

Director, Sales, Special Markets: Rita McMullen
Director, Sales, Premiums: Michael A. Peterson
Director, Sales, Retail: Tom Wierzbicki
Director, Book Marketing: Brad Elmitt
Director, Operations: George A. Susral
Director, Production: Douglas M. Johnston

Vice President and General Manager:
Douglas J. Guendel

Better Homes and Gardens® Magazine
Editor in Chief: Karol DeWulf Nickell

Meredith Publishing Group
President, Publishing Group: Stephen M. Lacy
Vice President-Publishing Director: Bob Mate

Meredith Corporation
Chairman and Chief Executive Officer: William T. Kerr

Chairman of the Executive Committee:
E. T. Meredith III

Copyright © 2002 by Meredith Corporation, Des Moines, Iowa. First Edition.
All rights reserved. Printed in the United States of America.
Library of Congress Control Number: 2002102023
ISBN: 0-696-21428-8

All of us at Better Homes and Gardens® Books are dedicated to providing you with information and ideas to create beautiful and useful projects. We welcome your comments and suggestions. Write to us at: Better Homes and Gardens Books, Crafts Editorial Department, 1716 Locust Street—LN112, Des Moines, IA 50309-3023.

If you would like to purchase any of our crafts, cooking, gardening, home improvement, or home decorating and design books, check wherever quality books are sold. Or visit us at: bhgbooks.com

Cover Photograph: Andy Lyons Cameraworks

Our seal assures you that every recipe in *Halloween Pumpkins & Parties* has been tested in the Better Homes and Gardens® Test Kitchen. This means that each recipe is practical and reliable, and meets our high standards of taste appeal. We guarantee your satisfaction with this book for as long as you own it.

Happy Halloween!

There's an autumn chill in the air and all eyes seem to be on you. Little spirits are running all around giggling about their tricks and asking for special treats. Bright orange pumpkins and ghoulish gourds line up on every porch and doorway just waiting to be transformed into works of art. Ideas for silly masks and scary costumes are filling your head as you plan that fiendish party with favorite friends. Ah yes, Halloween is upon us!

What other holiday allows us all to be so silly and have so much fun? Everyone from the very young to the very old can dress up to be someone they are not, eat Halloween goodies until they know they shouldn't, and decorate big orange gourds to look elaborate.

So, get scared! Get silly! Get in the spirit! Halloween is on its way and we're here to help make your **Pumpkins** and **Parties** the best ever! We've filled this "spooktacular" book chock-full of ideas for pumpkin carving, decorating, and displaying. We've given some "eeriesistable" recipes for you to make with all the tricks and treats for sure success. And we have "boo-tiful" costumes, treat bags, and decorations that the whole family can concoct together. Here's wishing you a frightfully-fun Halloween at your happily-haunted house!

Carol Field Dahlstrom

Carve Them Up

A departure from traditional jack-o'-lanterns, these fun pumpkin-carving ideas will have the neighborhood envying your creativity!

PAGES 8–29

Teeny, Tiny Pumpkins

Whether you want a quick accent or a painted treasure, miniature pumpkins can have a big impact on your Halloween decorating.

PAGES 30–39

Boo-tifully Decorated Pumpkins

From glass-beaded windows to Cinderella's carriage, you'll find wonderful new ways to decorate your bounty from the pumpkin patch.

PAGES 40–57

PARTIES
PAGES 58–143

TENTS

Decorate That Haunted House

Get ready for the haunting season in style with these irresistible trims for your home.
PAGES 60–97

Get the Goodies Ready

It just wouldn't be Halloween without fiendish foods to share with all your favorite goblins. **PAGES 98–115**

Get All Dressed Up

For something a bit more original than the store-bought variety, try make-it-yourself costumes, hats, and jewelry.
PAGES 116–131

Treat Them Right

When trick-or-treaters come knocking, surprise them with Halloween treats in spooktacular festive containers.
PAGES 132–143

PUMP

PUMPKINS

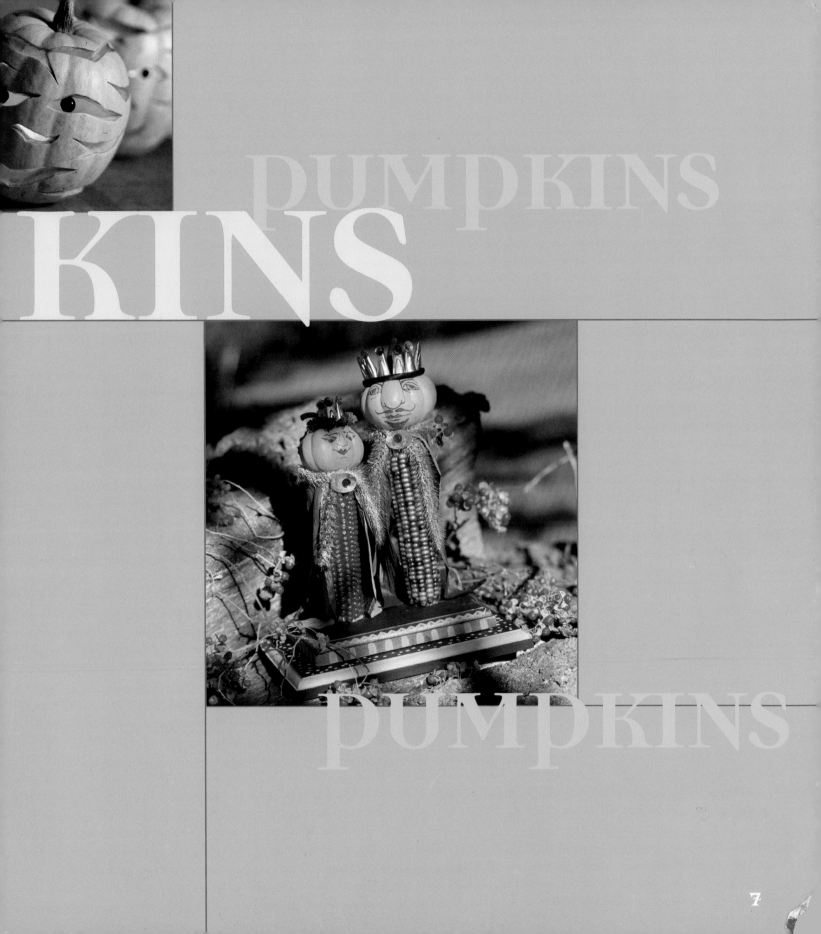

PUMPKINS
KINS

PUMPKINS

carve them up

Roll up your sleeves and get ready to create wonderfully carved pumpkins! Choose a Halloween motif or a scary face, carve it out, and let the candlelight shine through.

1 Cut off the top of the pumpkin. Scoop out.

2 Trace the spider pattern, above. Place the pattern on the pumpkin and slip a piece of transfer paper between the pumpkin and the pattern. Trace the pattern to transfer the lines to the pumpkin.

3 Carefully carve the pumpkin, following the pattern. Carve random lines around the spider, carving into the skin only.

4 Place a candle in the pumpkin. Replace the lid and light the candle through a carved area.

Note: **Never leave a burning candle unattended or in the reach of children.**

9

Call Me Mr. Mummy

This monster will have you wrapped with fear when his black piercing eyes stare at you.

WHAT YOU'LL NEED

Marking pen; paring knife
Smooth white pumpkins
Spoon or ice cream scoop
2 flat toothpicks
2 black marbles
Strong adhesive for glass,
    such as E6000
Candle

HERE'S HOW

1 Draw a line around pumpkin top. Cut off top as shown in Photo 1, right. Scoop out the insides as shown in Photo 2.

2 Cut the following slits using the photograph for inspiration: two for the eyes, wide and tall enough to accommodate the marbles; one for the end of the nose; and one for the mouth. Cut more slits around the gourd and on the edges of the lid.

3 Place a toothpick vertically into each eye opening in the gourd, where the marble is desired. Glue the marble to the toothpick. Let dry.

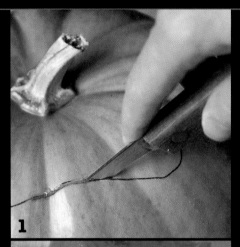

1

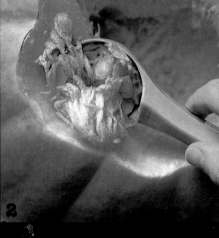

2

PUMPKIN-CARVING TIPS

Protect the work surface with newspapers or a plastic tablecloth. Cut off the top or bottom of the pumpkin, cutting a small notch for easy alignment. Scoop out the pumpkin using a strong spoon or ice cream scoop. Clean off the soft side of the lid as well. Carve carefully and slowly with a long, thin, sharp knife. Special pumpkin-cutting tools are also available wherever Halloween supplies are sold.

Note: **Never leave a burning candle unattended or in the reach of children.**

11

Headstone Engravings

Give your guests a graven greeting with a pair of frightful pumpkins.

WHAT YOU'LL NEED
Sharp knife
Pumpkin
Spoon or ice cream scoop
Tracing paper
Pencil
Transfer paper
Wood chisel

HERE'S HOW

1 Cut the pumpkin down both sides, leaving the front, back, and bottom intact. Scoop out the insides.

2 Enlarge and trace the desired pattern, below. Place the pattern on the pumpkin and slip a piece of transfer paper between the pumpkin and the pattern. Transfer the lines to the pumpkin.

3 Use the chisel to carve the desired designs into the skin of the pumpkin.

BOO PUMPKIN PATTERN   1 SQUARE = 1 INCH

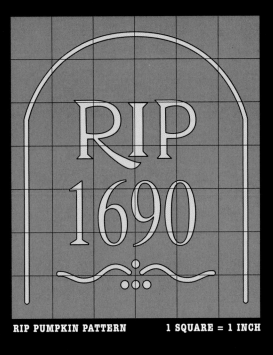

RIP PUMPKIN PATTERN   1 SQUARE = 1 INCH

Halloween Sky Pumpkin

Bats take flight around this pumpkin carved with a crescent moon and dancing stars.

WHAT YOU'LL NEED
Sharp knife; pumpkin
Spoon; tracing paper
Pencil; transfer paper
Wire screen; scissors
Straight pins; wire cutters
Heavyweight silver wire
Plastic bats

HERE'S HOW

1 Cut off the top of the pumpkin. Scoop out.

2 Trace the star and moon patterns, right and below. Place the patterns on the pumpkin and slip transfer paper between the pumpkin and the pattern. Trace the patterns to transfer the designs. Cut out the shapes.

3 Cut the screen ½ inch larger on all sides than the moon and large stars. Push the screen into the openings. To fill smaller stars, pin a piece of screen behind each cut star on the inside of the pumpkin.

4 Cut 3-foot lengths of wire and bend them into spirals. Anchor one end of each spiral in the pumpkin and hook a bat on the other end.

Note: **Never leave a burning candle unattended or in the reach of children.**

STAR PATTERNS

MOON PATTERNS

15

Monogram Pumpkins

Haunt your house in style with these handsome monogrammed pumpkins. If you have several pumpkins, spell out greetings to welcome all visitors.

WHAT YOU'LL NEED
Copy of monogram in
   desired size
Pumpkin; sharp knife
Spoon or ice cream scoop
Tape; pencil
Toothpicks
Candle

HERE'S HOW
1 Cut off the top of the pumpkin. Scoop out the insides.

2 Tape the copied monogram to the pumpkin surface. Lightly trace the monogram into the pumpkin's flesh. Remove the paper monogram.

3 Using a knife, carefully cut out the letter. To keep center parts suspended, such as the center of the R, insert several toothpicks around the piece and replace it securely in the pumpkin.

Note: **Never leave a burning candle unattended or in the reach of children.**

ABCDEFGHIJ
KLMNOPQRST
UVWXYZ

Creature Cutouts

Simple shapes carved into pumpkin shells make a bold Halloween statement.

WHAT YOU'LL NEED
Tracing paper; pencil
Scissors
Pumpkin, scooped out with lid cut
Paring knife
Sticks and twigs
26-gauge orange or black wire; wire cutters
Pumpkin-carving tools
Glass beads

instructions continued on page 21

18

Creature Cutouts

HERE'S HOW

1 To make any of the designs, trace the desired pattern, below or on pages 22–23. Cut out the pattern. Trace around the pattern on the pumpkin. Cut out the shape.

2 For the cat, make a broom by grouping a bunch of twigs around one end of a stick. Bind them in place by tightly winding wire six times around the twigs. Twist the wire ends together and trim the extra wire. To attach the broom, first poke a vertical pair of holes under each of the front cat paws. Hold the broom under the paws with one hand. With the other hand, secure it in place by threading a 3-inch length of wire out one hole, over the broom handle, and back in through the second hole. Twist the wire ends together inside the pumpkin. Repeat the process with the second pair of holes. Cut a 4-inch length of wire for the face. Thread a orange or black nose bead onto the center of the wire. Bend both wire ends up from the nose and then thread matching eye beads onto either side.

If necessary, bend the wire to secure the eye beads in place. Poke the wire ends into the pumpkin flesh on either side of the cat's head.

3 To make the owl, poke a vertical pair of holes under both owl wings. Follow the

instructions continued on page 22

CAT PUMPKIN PATTERN

21

directions for attaching the cat's broom to attach the owl's branch. Cut two 2-inch lengths of wire. Thread an eye bead onto the center of each wire. Bend the wire above and below the bead to hold it in place. Poke the wire ends into the pumpkin flesh at the top and bottom of eye sockets.

4 To make the bat, poke a pair of vertical holes above the bat's feet. Follow the directions for attaching the cat's broom to attach the branch above the bat's feet. With small beads and wire, make the bat's face as done for the cat's face.

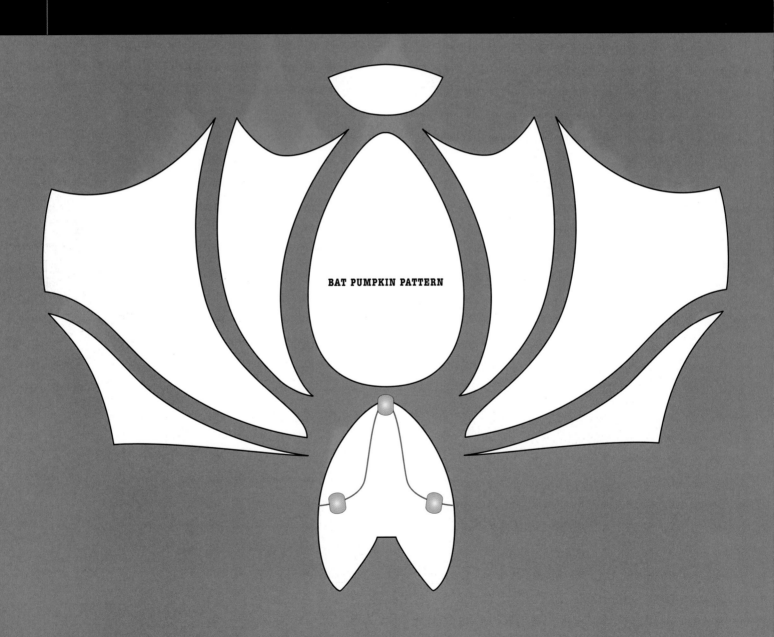

BAT PUMPKIN PATTERN

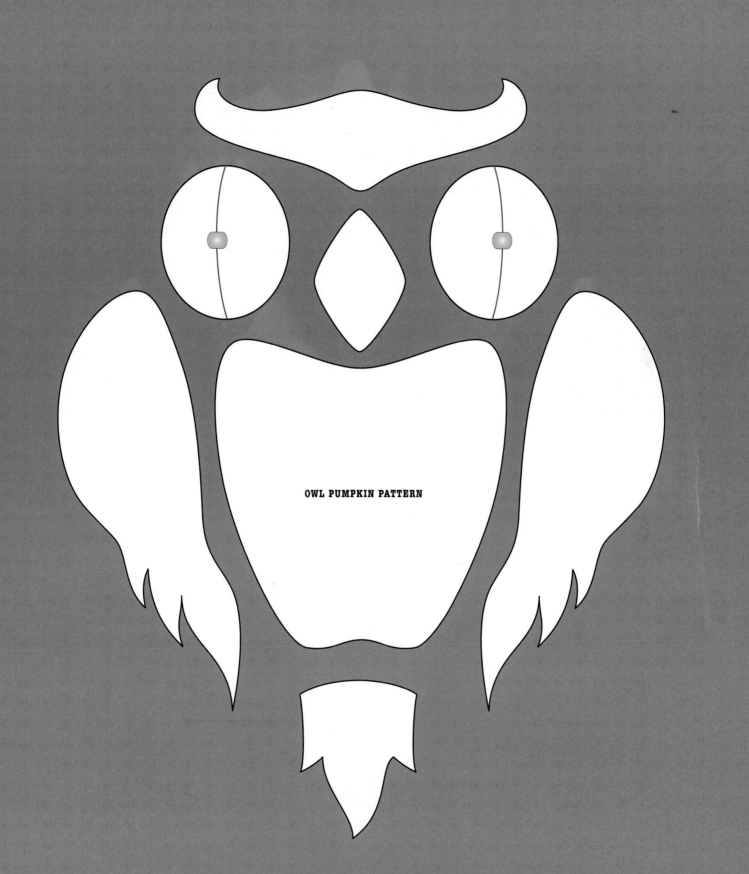

OWL PUMPKIN PATTERN

Pumpkins All Aglow

Grouping pumpkins near the front entry or in the garden makes frighteningly good holiday decor. Here traditional jack-o'-lanterns mingle with drilled pumpkins for a fun mix.

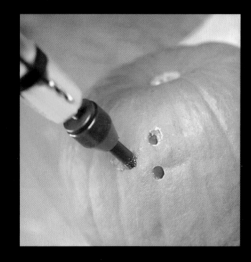

WHAT YOU'LL NEED

Pumpkins
Sharp knife
Spoon or ice cream scoop
Black latex paint and
    paintbrush, optional
Drill and drill bits in
    various sizes
White Christmas tree
    lights, candles, or
    battery-operated
    pumpkin lights
Tracing paper
Pencil
Transfer paper

HERE'S HOW

1 Cut off the top of each pumpkin. Scoop out.

2 To make a black pumpkin, paint the pumpkin skin with latex paint. Let it dry.

3 Drill a desired pattern or random holes in the pumpkin as shown above right. If using string lights, cut a small hole near the bottom of the pumpkin for the electrical cord. Place the light source in pumpkin.

4 To make a pumpkin with a carved face, enlarge and trace a pattern to the desired size from pages 26–27 or draw your own pattern on tracing paper. Place the pattern on the pumpkin and slip transfer paper between the pumpkin and the pattern.

Trace the lines. Carefully carve the pumpkin, following the drawn lines.

Note: **Never leave a burning candle unattended or in the reach of children.**

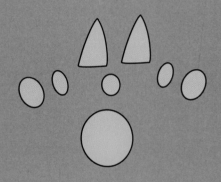
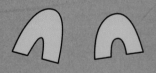

PUMPKIN FACE PATTERNS

26

PUMPKIN FACE PATTERNS

Willard the Warlock

Black iridescent marbles give this stern green fellow a spooky gaze.

WHAT YOU'LL NEED

Sharp knife
Green, orange, or
   white pumpkin
Spoon or ice cream scoop
Wood chisels
2 black iridescent marbles
2 yards of wire window
   screen
Ruler
Scissors
Stapler
18-inch length of
   1-inch-wide ribbon

HERE'S HOW

1 Cut off the top of the pumpkin. Scoop out the insides. Discard the lid.

2 Use a chisel to outline the warlock's eyes, nose, and mouth. Enlarge and deepen the initial carving until the desired look is achieved. Chisel wavy hair that comes down from the top of the head.

3 Cut circular pupils in the center of the warlock's eyes. Insert a marble into each hole.

4 Cut an 8-inch wide strip of screen off the 2-yard length. Set it aside to use for the brim of the hat. Fold the remaining screen in half and then roll it into a cone. Adjust the width of the base of the cone so it will fit on the warlock's pumpkin head.

Staple the overlapped edges together at the top and bottom of the cone. Fold down the top point of the hat and staple it in place. Fold the width of the eight inch strip in half and staple it to around the base of the cone, gathering it together whenever necessary. Trim off any extra brim. Tie a ribbon around the brim to make a hatband.

teeny, tiny pumpkins

Small enough to hold in the palm of your hand, miniature pumpkins make a big impact on your Halloween table.

Metallic Mini

Frosted with a light coat of red metallic spray paint, this little pumpkin shines with color. A simple ribbon bow adds an elegant touch.

WHAT YOU'LL NEED
Newspapers
Red metallic spray paint
Miniature pumpkin
¼-inch-wide golden metallic ribbon
Scissors; ruler

HERE'S HOW

1 In a well-ventilated work area, cover the work surface with newspapers. Spray the pumpkin top with red metallic paint. Let dry.

2 Cut a 12-inch-long piece of ribbon. Tie into a bow around the pumpkin stem. Trim the ribbon ends as desired.

Pumpkinland Royalty

Add an unexpected touch to your Halloween decorating with a playful King and Queen crafted from miniature pumpkins and colorful corn.

WHAT YOU'LL NEED

Newspapers
White spray primer
5×7- and 6½×9-inch beveled wood pieces
Acrylic paints in black, yellow, orange, lime green, purple, grass green, and magenta
Medium flat paintbrush and fine liner paintbrush
Thick white crafts glue
2 ears of colored corn
Water; bleach
Scissors; knife
2 small pumpkins, real or artificial
Drill and small drill bit
Two 3-inch screws
Hot-glue gun; glue sticks
Foxtail grass or similar dried flowers
Assorted gems
Tracing paper and soft lead pencil
Black permanent marker
Candy corn
Gold tone spray paint
Black braid trim

HERE'S HOW

1 In a well-ventilated work area, cover work surface with newspapers. Spray one side of each wood piece and the edges with white primer. Let the paint dry. Turn the wood pieces over and apply spray primer.

2 Paint the top surfaces of the wood pieces black. Using the photograph, opposite, for inspiration, add orange and purple borders, yellow dots, magenta stripes, and lime green wavy lines. To paint dots, dip the handle of a paintbrush into paint and dot onto surface.

3 Glue the smaller wood piece in the center of the larger piece. Let the glue dry.

4 To prepare the ears of corn, carefully remove husks, keeping them intact. To soften and clean the husks, mix ¼ cup bleach and 1 gallon water. Soak the husks in the bleach water 10 minutes. Separate each piece so they are easier to work with. Dab off excess water.

5 Trim the damp, pliable husks to the desired length. Trim the outer husks shorter than the inner husks. Paint the husks using purple, magenta, lime green, and grass green. Paint stems of the pumpkins green. Shape the husks back into their original shape and let dry. Cut the ends of each ear of corn so they are flat.

6 Drill two holes in the bottom of the wood piece where you want the ears of corn to stand. Insert screws into the wood piece and screw on the ears of corn.

instructions continued on page 34

7 Reattach the painted husks to the corn in layers using hot glue. Decorate with foxtail grass or dried flowers and gems.

8 Trace the face patterns, right, or make your own on tracing paper. Color the back of each tracing paper with a soft lead pencil. Place the patterns on the pumpkins and trace the pattern lines to transfer the drawings. Darken the pencil lines by drawing over them with a black marker.

9 Hot-glue the pumpkin heads on top of the corn.

10 In a well-ventilated work area, cover the work surface with newspapers. Spray the candy corn with gold spray paint. Let dry. Hot-glue the candy corn onto the pumpkin heads in shape of a crown. Hot-glue gems to the crown tips. Glue black braid trim around the base of each crown.

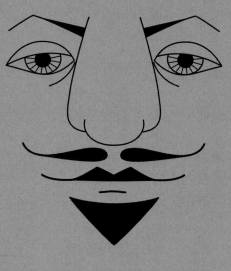

KING'S FACE PATTERN

QUEEN'S FACE PATTERN

Pumpkins in a Row

Nestled in chunky lavender bath salts, these pumpkins are transformed into enticing candleholders. Change the bath salts and taper candles to seasonal colors and this arrangement can be enjoyed all year long.

WHAT YOU'LL NEED
Miniature pumpkins
Sharp knife
Taper candles
Lavender bath salts
Shallow container, such as a planter or serving dish

HERE'S HOW

1 Cut a hole in the top of each pumpkin, just large enough to fit the taper candle.

2 Fill the container two-thirds of the way with bath salts. Arrange the pumpkins in the salt, pushing down gently to make secure.

3 Place a candle in each pumpkin. Add a pinch of bath salt around the base of each candle.

Note: **Never leave a burning candle unattended or in the reach of children.**

Rustic Candelabra

Fashion an outdoor pumpkin candelabra from an antique wooden garden rake. Suspend the pumpkins in place with wire hangers.

WHAT YOU'LL NEED
Rake
Sharp knife
Miniature pumpkins
Votive candles
Metal skewer or ice pick
18-gauge wire
Wire cutters

HERE'S HOW

1 Secure the rake handle in the ground.

2 Cut the tops off the pumpkins. Discard the lids. Cut out areas large enough to accommodate a votive candle.

3 Using a metal skewer or ice pick, punch two or three small holes around the top edge of the pumpkin.

4 Cut two or three equal lengths of 18-gauge wire. Thread one through each hole, twisting to secure. Bring the loose ends of wire together and loop around the rake tines. Twist to secure. Insert a candle in each pumpkin.

Note: **Never leave a burning candle unattended or in the reach of children.**

Greet guests with a wreath that sets the stage for Halloween fun.

Pumpkin Ring Wreath

WHAT YOU'LL NEED
Drill and ⁹⁄₆₄-inch drill bit
Miniature pumpkins
20-gauge aluminum wire
Wire cutters
Wire wreath form
    (available at crafts and
    floral supply stores)
Dry moss
2-inch-wide ribbon
Scissors

HERE'S HOW

1 Drill a hole through each miniature pumpkin (side to side), positioning the holes toward the bottom of the pumpkin where they won't be very visible.

2 String a piece of wire through the openings in one pumpkin. Place pumpkin on a wire wreath form so wires are perpendicular to the form.

Bring wires around to the back of the form and twist them to secure to the form. Continue wiring pumpkins to the form until it is covered. Fill the spaces between the pumpkins with dry moss by wiring it to the form.

3 Tie a generous bow from ribbon. Wire to the top of the wreath. Trim the ribbon ends.

Glitter Glamour

1 Cover the work surface with newspapers.

2 For the striped pumpkin, paint glue stripes on a pumpkin. Sprinkle glitter over the wet glue. Let the glue dry. Shake off the excess glitter.

3 For the boo pumpkin, stamp the word BOO randomly on a clean, dry pumpkin. Let dry. Put a dot of glue in the center of the Os and sprinkle with glitter. Let dry.

4 Cut 12-inch lengths of metallic thread or ribbon. Tie around the pumpkin stem. Trim ends as desired.

With a little glue and glitter you can make these glistening beauties quicker than you can say, "Pretty, Pretty Pumpkin!"

WHAT YOU'LL NEED FOR THE BOO AND STRIPED PUMPKINS

Newspapers
Miniature pumpkin
Small paintbrush
White glue; glitter
Rubber alphabet stamps
Black stamp pad
Metallic thread or ribbon
Scissors

Use a pencil eraser to add dots of glue to the pumpkin and sprinkle with glitter for a sparkling effect. When using two colors, dot enough glue on for one color, add glitter, and repeat for the second color.

Pretty Polka Dots

WHAT YOU'LL NEED
Newspapers
Miniature pumpkin
Pencil with eraser
White glue
Small paintbrush
Glitter
Metallic embroidery
   thread
Scissors

HERE'S HOW

1 Cover the work surface with newspapers.

2 Using the eraser end of the pencil, make dots of glue on the pumpkin. Use a paintbrush to paint the stem with glue. While the glue is wet, sprinkle with glitter. Let dry. Shake off the excess glitter.

3 Cut four 12-inch lengths of thread. Tie into a bow around the pumpkin stem. Trim the ends if needed.

boo-tifully decorated pumpkins

Plain pumpkins, step aside! These cleverly decorated pumpkins will knock your Halloween socks right off! From elegantly beaded windows to playful nut characters, you'll get oodles of ideas in this fun-filled chapter.

Jeweled Pumpkin

For an elegant pumpkin that shimmers with color, display glass beads in diamond-shape windows trimmed with upholstery tacks.

WHAT YOU'LL NEED
Pumpkin
Sharp knife
Spoon or ice cream scoop
Tracing paper
Pencil
Scissors
Crafting wire
Wire cutters; ruler
Assorted translucent
    colored glass beads
1½-inch eye pins
Upholstery tacks

HERE'S HOW
1 Cut off the bottom of the pumpkin. Scoop out.

2 Trace the diamond pattern, page 42. Cut out.

3 Trace around the diamond pattern on the pumpkin vertically three or more times. Cut out the shapes using a knife.

4 For each center beaded row, cut a 5½-inch piece of wire. Thread beads on wire in desired arrangement. Poke one end of the beaded wire into the bottom of the diamond. Bend the wire slightly to

instructions continued
on page 42

enable the top of the wire to be inserted into the top of the diamond as shown in Photo 1, right.

5 For each short beaded row, thread beads on an eye pin. As shown in Photo 2, poke the straight end of the pin into the top of the diamond, one on each side of the center row.

6 Push an upholstery tack into the pumpkin at each point of the diamond. Add an upholstery tack between each point.

DIAMOND PATTERN

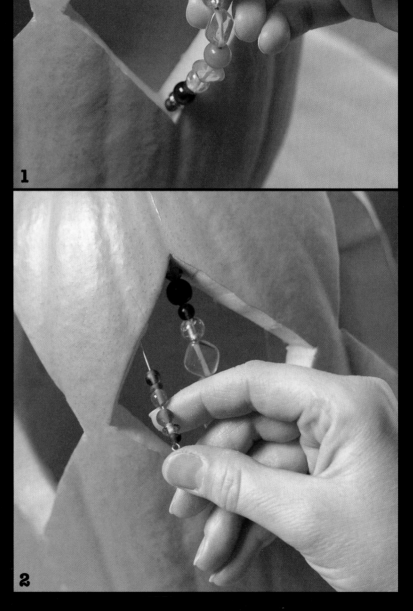

1

2

Create a vivacious pumpkin full of personality with these nutty little characters.

Little Critter Lodge

WHAT YOU'LL NEED

Tall pumpkin; marking pen
Knife; spoon; thick pink craft foam; scissors
Thick white crafts glue
Acorns, pecans, English walnut, almonds, chestnuts, pistachios, and allspice
Glossy acrylic paints in desired colors; paintbrush
Pipe cleaners; toothpicks

HERE'S HOW

1 Using the photo for ideas, draw a door and windows on the pumpkin. Cut out a circular shape from the bottom of pumpkin. Scoop out the insides. Cut out the shapes.

2 From craft foam, cut rectangular shutters with one rounded corner. Draw shutter lines with a marking pen. Glue shutters by window openings.

3 To make critters, glue nuts together. Use half a walnut shell with an almond to make the door critter. Use allspice for eyes and noses. Draw details with marking pen. Use pistachio shells for the ears. When glue is dry, paint as desired. Paint stem green. Let dry. For the door critter, glue on pipe cleaner arms and legs. Use toothpicks to support critters if needed.

The Pumpkin King

Crown this no-carve king with a collar that's normally used in ductwork.

WHAT YOU'LL NEED
Tracing paper; pencil
Pumpkin
Permanent markers in
  black, blue, and white
6-inch start collar with
  crimp (found with the
  aluminum ductwork
  supplies in hardware and
  home center stores)
Strong adhesive, such
  as E6000
Gems in assorted sizes,
  shapes, and colors

HERE'S HOW

1 Enlarge and trace the pattern, below. Place the pattern on the pumpkin, pencil side down. Trace over the lines (they should show through the back) to transfer the pattern.

2 Outline the pattern lines with black marker. Color in the eyes using blue. Color in the whites of the eyes. Let the marker lines dry.

3 Glue gems around the start collar as desired. Let the glue dry. Place the crown on the pumpkin.

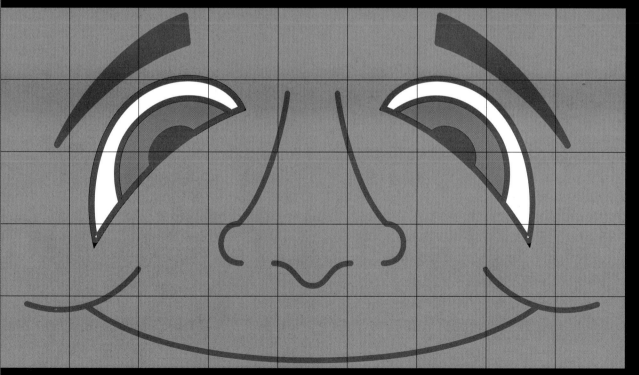

THE PUMPKIN KING FACE PATTERN

1 SQUARE = 1 INCH

Finial Pumpkin Stems

Use these striking pumpkin stems year after year. Simply unscrew the stems and save them for the next haunting season.

WHAT YOU'LL NEED
Utility knife; pumpkins
Scrap piece of board
Drill and ⅛-inch drill bit
Fence post finials
Newspapers
White spray primer
Acrylic paints in black,
    white, orange, purple,
    green, and yellow
Paintbrushes
Glossy acrylic sealer

HERE'S HOW

1 Using a utility knife, cut the stem off each pumpkin, cutting as close to the pumpkin as possible.

2 To keep finials upright while painting, drill holes in a scrap piece of board, leaving at least 6 inches between holes. Screw the finials into the board until secure.

3 In a well-ventilated work area, cover the work surface with newspapers. Spray a coat of primer on the finials. Let the paint dry.

4 Paint each finial white or black. Let dry.

5 Using the photograph, opposite, for ideas, paint various colored checks, dots, swirls, or other desired motifs on the finials. Let the paint dry.

6 Paint a coat of acrylic sealer on each finial. Let the sealer dry. Paint on a second coat and let dry.

7 Screw a finial into the top of the pumpkin where the stem was removed.

Haunted Pumpkin on Boo Avenue

Fit for ghouls of every sort, this miniature mansion makes a most haunting centerpiece.

WHAT YOU'LL NEED
Tracing paper; pencil
Scissors
Heavy black paper; ruler
⅛-inch square dowel; saw
Thick white crafts glue
Acrylic paints in purple, green, orange, and white
Paintbrush
Alphabet macaroni
4-inch-long metal banner and a 1½-inch-wide metal sign (available with the miniatures in crafts stores)
Medium-size pumpkin
Brush-on white glitter
8-inch foam wreath
Assorted dried flowers
Miniature tree (available in crafts shops with the miniature village items)

HERE'S HOW

1 Trace the patterns, right. Cut out. Trace the shapes on black paper and cut out. Cut an 8½×5½-inch piece of black paper for roof.

2 Cut pieces of dowel to frame and add crossbars to each window and door. Glue in place. Let dry.

3 Paint the dowel pieces purple. Let dry. Add green stripes. Let dry. Paint orange checks along the edge of the roof. Let dry.

4 Glue alphabet macaroni onto the banner to spell BOO AVENUE. Glue the word BEWARE on the sign. Glue an O on the door for the doorknob. Let dry.

5 Paint the macaroni white. Add green shading to letters. Paint doorknob orange. Let dry.

6 Glue the door, windows, and BOO AVENUE banner to one side of the pumpkin. Let dry.

7 Fold the roof piece in half. Cut an X in the center to slip over the stem. Pleat roof once on each side of fold as shown in photo. Place over stem.

8 Paint glitter on the stem, roof, and pumpkin. Let dry.

9 Place pumpkin in wreath. Cover wreath by poking in dried flowers. Add the BEWARE sign and miniature tree.

DOOR PATTERN

SMALL WINDOW PATTERN

LARGE WINDOW PATTERN

Cinderelly's Carriage

Birthday candles light the way for this storybook creation.

WHAT YOU'LL NEED

Short, wide pumpkin
Sharp knife
Spoon or ice cream scoop
Pencil; tracing paper
Scissors
Cardboard; utility knife
Newspapers
Gold spray paint
Gold dimensional glitter
   paint; gold braid
Thick white crafts glue
Upholstery tacks
Birthday cake
   candleholders
Wood disk approximately
   3 inches across
Wood heart approximately
   2½ inches high
2 decorative wood pegs
Small piece of gold fringe
Birthday candles

HERE'S HOW

1 Use a sharp knife to cut a circular shape on top of pumpkin and remove the lid. Scoop out the insides of the pumpkin.

2 Use a pencil to draw in arched windows and to mark the position of the wheels and seat. Cut out the windows. Cut an opening for a door on the back of the pumpkin if desired.

3 Trace the wheel pattern, page 52, onto tracing paper. Cut out and trace onto cardboard twice. Cut out the cardboard shapes.

4 In a well-ventilated work area, cover the work surface with newspapers. Spray-paint the wheels gold. Let dry. Paint gold glitter onto the wheels. Let dry. Glue gold braid around each wheel. Secure each wheel in place with an upholstery tack.

instructions continued
on page 52

5 Trim all the openings with gold braid. Hold in place with tacks.

6 Spray-paint the candleholders and the wood pieces gold. Let dry. Glue gold fringe to the wood disk.

7 Cut an area just large enough to fit the round wood disk and insert into pumpkin. Cut into pumpkin to insert the heart-shaped back. Insert two wood pegs.

8 Insert the candleholders with candles on each side of the windows.

Note: **Never leave a burning candle unattended or in the reach of children.**

WHEEL PATTERN

Party Pumpkin

Embellish a purchased party hat with black and orange rickrack for instant Halloween pizzazz. Make them for guests or for your favorite jack-o'-lantern.

WHAT YOU'LL NEED
Tape measure
Pencil
Party hat
Paper punch
Eyelet tool
Black eyelets
Rickrack in orange
   and black
Fine gold wire
Hot-glue gun; glue sticks
Ribbon
Pumpkin
White glue
Glitter

HERE'S HOW

1 Measuring ½ inch from the base of the party hat, mark every inch. Punch holes at marks. Glue a piece of black rickrack on the inside edge of the hat.

2 Secure an eyelet at each hole. Cut 12-inch lengths of rickrack. Knot one end of each length. From inside hat, thread alternating colors of rickrack through the bottom holes. Gather rickrack at the top and wrap with wire to secure at point of hat.

Add a ribbon tie through each of two opposite holes.

3 For pumpkin, draw a face with glue. Sprinkle desired colors of glitter over wet glue. Let dry and shake off excess glitter.

Creepin' Cat Pumpkin

This clever pumpkin made of foam will last for many eerie Halloweens to come.

WHAT YOU'LL NEED
Sharp knife; foam pumpkin
Wood-carving tools; scissors
Tracing paper; pencil
Awl; plastic animal eyes
Black acrylic paint
Paintbrush; black marker
Black craft foam; ruler
Straight pins; gold wire

HERE'S HOW

1 Cut off the top of the pumpkin and discard the lid. Invert the pumpkin so the cut opening rests on your work surface. Trim the opening if it doesn't sit flat.

2 Poke two holes in the top front of the pumpkin and insert the plastic animal eyes through the holes.

3 Enlarge and trace the patterns, right. Cut out the shapes. Using a marker, outline the cat's body on the pumpkin. Fill in the outline with black paint. Using the photograph, opposite, as a guide, cut out pieces of the pumpkin to make the cat design stand out.

4 Cut two V-shape slits above the cat's eyes. Cut out black foam ears and a tail. Insert the base of the ears into the slits. Pin the cat's tail in place. Poke in 5-inch wire whiskers.

CAT FRONT PATTERN   1 SQUARE = 1 INCH

CAT BACK PATTERN   1 SQUARE = 1 INCH

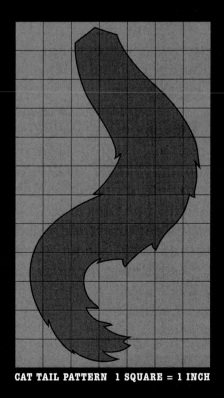

CAT TAIL PATTERN 1 SQUARE = 1 INCH

CAT EAR PATTERN
1 SQUARE = 1 INCH

55

Peter, Peter Pumpkin Keeper

A popular nursery rhyme cleverly adorns this carve-and-paint pumpkin.

WHAT YOU'LL NEED
Large pumpkin
Pencil
Knife
Scraper
Wide paint markers in
    purple, turquoise,
    and black
Air-dry clay, such as
    Crayola Model Magic
Acrylic paints in blue,
    white, orange, black,
    gray, and red
Paintbrush
Raffia
Straight pins
Thick white crafts glue
Foam
Drawer pull
Fencing staples
Miniature garden hoe

HERE'S HOW

1 Wash and dry the pumpkin. Referring to the photograph, opposite, use a pencil to draw the lettering and door where desired. Make the lines wavy.

2 Cut out door shape. Cut out windowpanes. Scrape out the insides of the pumpkin.

3 Draw the words boldly using paint markers. Alternate the colors on each row. Add a black shadow to one side and to the bottom of each letter.

4 To make clay birds, shape a round head with neck and attach it to another round body shape. Form a small cone and cut down the center for the beak. Attach to the head.

Let dry. Paint birds blue, eyes white, and pupils black. Paint beaks orange.

5 Wind a handful of raffia into a nest and place on top of pumpkin. Pin and glue nest and birds in place.

6 For the chimney, cut a piece of foam into a small rectangle. Paint gray, let dry, and paint in red bricks. Let dry. Pin in place on top of pumpkin.

7 Press drawer pull into door. Insert the ends only of two staples, one on the door and one on the pumpkin wall. Insert hoe through the staples.

PARTIES

PARTIES

decorate
that haunted house

Show your Halloween spirit indoors and out with handcrafted decorations to make all ghostly guests feel welcome. With innovative ideas in this chapter, you'll transform your home into a haunted house. For instructions and patterns for streamers, see page 97.

Beaded Candle Cuff

Let the colors of Halloween shine through with glass beads in purple, orange, black, green, and yellow. Dangle them from a wire zigzag that hugs the top of a candleholder.

WHAT YOU'LL NEED

Brass wire
Wire cutters; ruler
Candle in round glass
    candleholder
1½-inch-long gold eye pins
Glass beads in purple,
    orange, black, green,
    and yellow
Needlenose pliers

HERE'S HOW

1 Cut a 16-inch length of wire; bend the wire into a strip of zigzags, each about 1 inch high.

2 Align the center of the zigzags with the rim of the candleholder. Fold the wire zigzags over the candleholder edge. Trim excess wire.

3 Place one to three beads on an eye pin. Using needlenose pliers, bend the end of the eye pin. Hook the eye pin onto the wire zigzag. Using the pliers, close the opening in the eye pin to secure. Continue working in this manner until a beaded pin is hanging from each wire zigzag loop on the outside of the candleholder.

Note: **Never leave a burning candle unattended or in the reach of children.**

Witchy Welcome Sign

Hanging from a witch's broom, these words of warning are perfect for the entrance of any haunted house.

WHAT YOU'LL NEED

Broom with wood handle
Medium-grit sandpaper
Tack cloth; newspapers
Spray paints in silver
   and purple; scissors
Acrylic enamel paints in
   black and orange
1- and ½-inch flat brushes
Tracing paper; pencil; ruler
2×4-foot piece of plywood
Band saw
Acrylic paints in white,
   black, bright green,
   purple, and bright orange
Crackle medium
Transfer paper
Drill and ¹⁄₁₆-inch bit
6 small eye screws
6 feet of chain

HERE'S HOW

1 Sand broom handle and wipe with tack cloth. In a well-ventilated work area, cover work surface with newspapers. Spray-paint the broom bristles silver. Shade as desired with purple. Let dry.

2 Use a pencil and ruler to mark broom handle in 2-inch increments. Paint alternating black and orange stripes around broom handle using the marks as guides. Let dry.

3 Enlarge and trace the sign pattern and lettering, below. Cut out the sign shape. Draw around the sign shape on plywood. Cut out. Sand and wipe edges.

4 Paint the sign using white acrylic. Let dry. Apply a thick coat of crackle medium to the front of the sign. Let dry. Paint over the crackle medium with black acrylic, trying not to overlap brushstrokes. Let dry.

5 Paint the edges of the sign silver. Let dry.

6 Use transfer paper to transfer the lettering to the wood sign. Using the pattern as a guide, paint the letters with acrylic paints. Add green and orange shading to the edges of the sign. Let dry.

7 Drill two ¹⁄₁₆-inch holes in the top and bottom of the broom handle and in the top of the sign as shown in the photo, opposite. Screw an eye screw into each hole. Attach chain pieces to each of the eye screws.

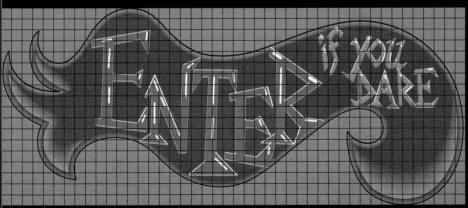

WITCHY WELCOME SIGN PATTERN   1 SQUARE = 1 INCH

Creepy Coasters

With spiders dangling from the corners, these spiderweb coasters dress up a Halloween table in style.

WHAT YOU'LL NEED
Tracing paper
Pencil; scissors
Black crafting
  foam
Pearl white
  tube-style paint
⅛-inch paper punch
Thin black elastic cord
Black plastic spiders

HERE'S HOW

1 Trace the pattern, right. Cut out the shape. Trace around the pattern as many times as desired on black foam. Cut out shapes.

2 Using paint, make an irregular spiderweb on one side of each foam web shape. Starting in the center of the web, make seven spokes that extend to the edge of the coaster. Connect the spokes with uneven lines. Let the paint dry overnight.

3 Punch one hole along the edge of each coaster. Cut a 4- to 6-inch length of elastic for each coaster. Tie one end of the elastic to a spider and then tie the other end through the punched hole in the coaster.

COASTER PATTERN

Frightful Lights

Quick cutouts add Halloween flair to purchased lampshades.

WHAT YOU'LL NEED
Tracing paper; pencil
Scissors; paper lampshades
Decoupage medium
Paintbrush; straight pin
Black braid trim
Hot-glue gun; glue sticks

For the bat:
Black tissue paper
Gold art paper; white wire

For the cat:
Black tissue paper
24-gauge gold wire
Rhinestones in amber and
   black; needlenose pliers
Thick white crafts glue

For the spider:
White lace art paper; white
   wire; black plastic spider
Black permanent marker

HERE'S HOW
1 Glue braid trim to shade as desired. Trace the desired pattern, pages 68–69. Cut out shape.

2 Trace around pattern on the desired tissue and/or art paper. Cut out.

Use photo, below, as a guide, to cut a spiderweb.

3 Brush a thin layer of decoupage medium on the back of each cutout. Place the wet side of the cutout onto the lampshade.

4 For the cat, cut four ½- to 1-inch-long wire whiskers. Use needlenose pliers to spiral one end of each whisker. Apply a small amount of glue to the straight ends of two of the whiskers and then tuck them between the cat's cheek and the lampshade. Use a straight pin to poke two holes through the other cheek. Push the remaining two whiskers through the holes. To hold the whiskers in place, reach inside the lampshade and fold the wire ends over.

5 Glue two amber rhinestone eyes and a black rhinestone nose onto the cat's face.

instructions continued on page 68

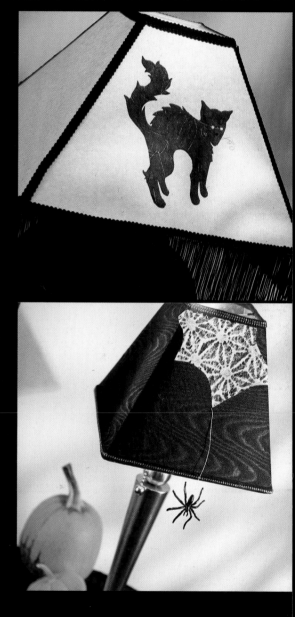

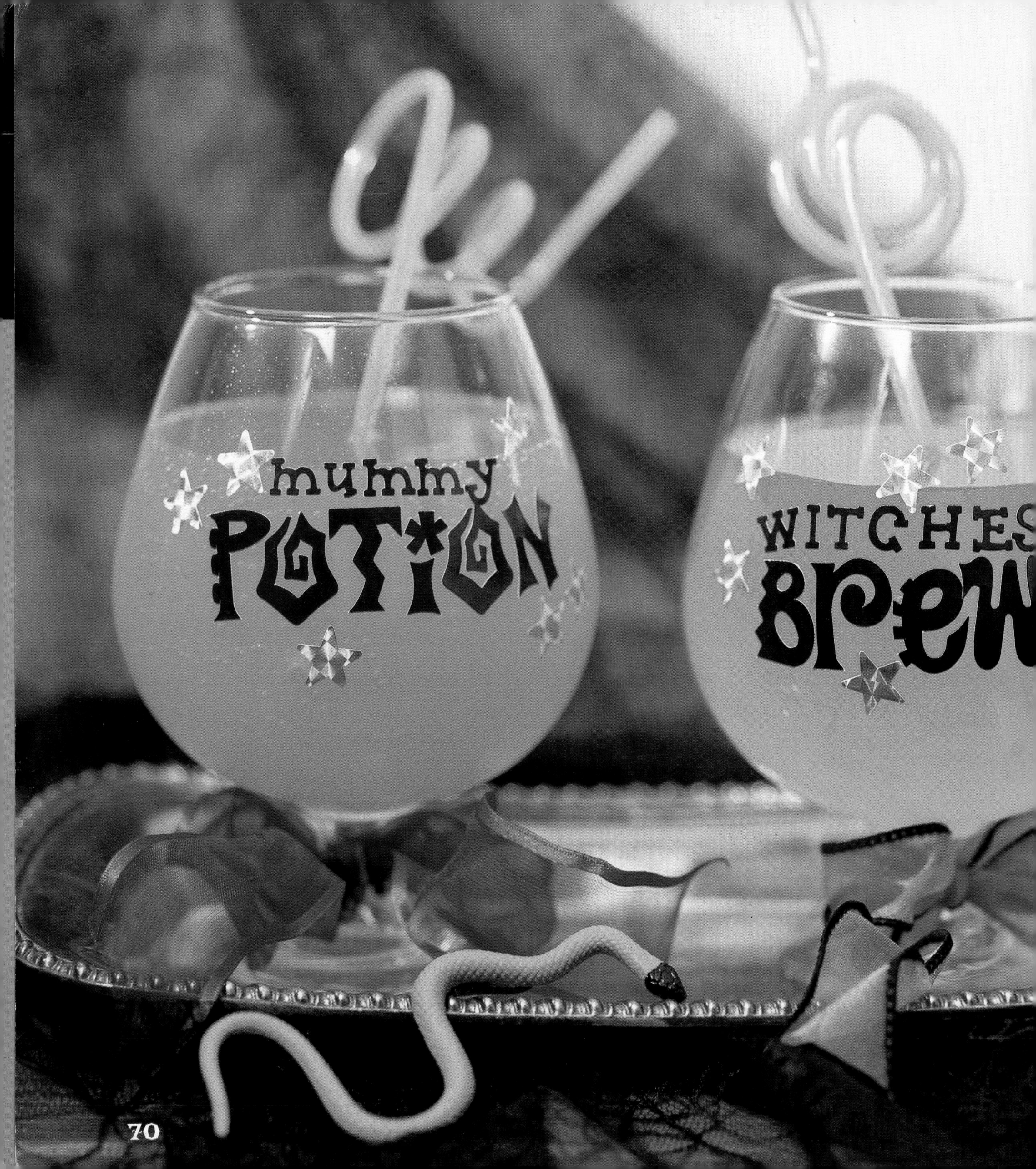
mummy
POTION
WITCHES
BREW

Goblin Goblets

These generous glasses are perfect for a jumbo serving of chilled Halloween potion. The sticker designs go on quick as a bat, so you can make one for each guest at your gruesome gathering.

WHAT YOU'LL NEED

Clear glass goblets

3/8- and 1-inch black letter stickers (available in the scrapbooking section of crafts stores)

1/2-inch metallic silver star stickers

1- to 1 1/2-inch-wide wire-edge ribbon

Scissors

HERE'S HOW

1 Wash and dry the goblets. Avoid touching the surface where the stickers will be attached.

2 Decide on letter placement. Starting with large letters, peel and apply to goblet spelling the word **BREW** or **POTION**.

3 Center and apply the small letters above the first, spelling the word **WITCHES'** or **MUMMY**.

4 Press star stickers randomly around the lettering, keeping away from the rim of the glass.

5 Cut an 18-inch length of ribbon. Tie the ribbon into a bow around the stem of the goblet. Trim the ribbon ends.

Staring Silverware

Watch what you say and what you do.
When you eat with these weird utensils,
all eyes are on you!

WHAT YOU'LL NEED

Black polymer clay, such
   as Premo Sculpey
Stainless-steel silverware
Small and large flat-backed
   blue plastic doll eyes
Strong adhesive, such as
   E6000, optional

HERE'S HOW

1 Soften one-third of the polymer clay square by working it in your hands. Flatten the clay with your fingertips until it is $\frac{1}{8}$ to $\frac{1}{4}$ inch thick.

2 Wrap the clay around the handle of a silverware piece and then pinch off any excess. Squeeze the wrapped handle to remove any air pockets and to ensure the clay is tightly connected. Smooth away any overlaps or dings with your fingertips. Firmly press doll eyes into the front and back of the clay-covered handle.

3 Bake the decorated silverware according to polymer clay package directions. Let cool. If any of the doll eyes loosen or fall out after baking, glue them back in place and let dry.

4 Carefully hand wash silverware after use. Try to avoid dropping or banging hardened polymer clay, as it may chip or break.

74

Wired Welcome Web

Start the party off right with a tangled arachnid door decoration.

WHAT YOU'LL NEED

Pruning shears
Forked branch
Acrylic paints in black, silver, or gold
½-inch flat paintbrush
Glitter
24-gauge orange, black, or gold wire; wire cutters
Beaded or large plastic spider
Thick white crafts glue
Glitter puff paint, optional

HERE'S HOW

1 Use pruning shears to trim the branch ends. Paint the branch with the desired color of paint. Sprinkle glitter onto the wet paint and let the branch dry.

2 Cut six or seven 12- to 15-inch lengths of wire. Wrap one end of a wire piece around one side of the forked branch. Position the center of the wire where you would like the middle of the web. Wrap the other end of the wire to the opposite branch. Repeat the process with the remaining wires until all the spokes of the web are positioned.

3 Cut a 16-inch length of wire. Wrap the end of the wire around one of the spokes. Work the other end of the wire around each spoke of the web until a complete spiral is achieved. Poke the end of the wire into the spider and then glue it in place.

4 If desired, add dewdrops of puff paint to the spiderweb and then let dry before hanging.

Party Pal Piñata

The expression on this skeleton's face looks as though he knows the candy is about to be knocked out of him.

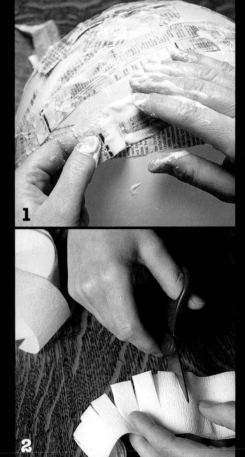

WHAT YOU'LL NEED
15-inch balloon; 1 cup flour
Cold water; 2 bowls
Newspaper strips; ice pick
Candy; pipe cleaners
White crepe paper
Scissors; glue stick
Tracing paper; pencil
Construction paper in
   white, black, and red
Wide black marker
Plastic top hat
Reinforcement stickers in
   purple and white
Silver star stickers
1½-inch-wide orange ribbon
Feathers in black, white,
   orange, purple, and green
Screen door spring

HERE'S HOW
1 Blow up the balloon until firm and knot.

2 In a bowl, mix flour with enough cold water to make a thick paste. Dip a newspaper strip into the flour paste. Pull paper strip between fingers to remove any excess paste. Apply the paper strip to the balloon.

Continue adding strips in this manner, overlapping pieces and applying in various directions as shown in Photo 1, right. Add paper strips until there are four or five layers covering the entire balloon. Let dry.

3 Cut a small hole where the eye will be placed. Fill the piñata with candy through hole. Use an ice pick to poke two holes in the large end of the piñata. Thread pipe cleaner through holes and twist to secure.

4 Cut 3-yard lengths of crepe paper and loop into a small ring. Cut a fringe on one side, leaving at least ¼ inch uncut as shown in Photo 2.

5 Beginning at knotted end of balloon, start wrapping crepe paper around balloon, fringe side down. Use glue stick to secure crepe paper in place, overlapping crepe paper as necessary to cover newspaper on balloon.

6 Trace the patterns, pages 78–79. Cut out. Trace around eyebrows, eyes nose, and bow tie on black. Trace mouth and pupils on white. Trace eyes on red. Cut out shapes. Draw in teeth with marker.

7 Use glue stick to adhere the facial features onto

instructions continued on page 78

Halloween Hurricane

Light up your own miniature Halloween sky with this hurricane shade painted with a witch in flight.

WHAT YOU'LL NEED
Hurricane shade
Tracing paper
Pencil
Scissors
Tape
Fine-point permanent
  black pen, such as Pigma
Oven-bake glass paints in
  black and yellow
Paintbrushes
Fingernail polish remover,
  toothpick, and crafts
  knife, optional

HERE'S HOW

1 Wash and dry the hurricane shade. Avoid touching the areas to be painted.

2 Trace the patterns, pages 82–83. Cut out. Tape patterns onto glass and trace around them with the black pen. Do not trace the stars and vines. Remove the patterns. Paint the moon and pumpkin eyes yellow. Paint the remaining designs black. Several coats of paint are necessary. Allow to dry between coats.

3 Use black pen to draw stars and vines. Paint over the lines with black paint. Any visible pen lines can be removed by dipping end of a toothpick into fingernail polish remover and then applying to unwanted lines. Unwanted paint can be removed by using a crafts knife. Bake the hurricane in the oven, if necessary, according to the paint manufacturer's directions. Let cool.

Note: **Never leave a burning candle unattended or in the reach of children.**

HALLOWEEN HURRICANE WITCH PATTERN

HALLOWEEN HURRICANE PUMPKIN PATTERNS

Drinks à la Decoupage

Make a different goblet base for every guest using an assortment of papers in Halloween colors and designs.

WHAT YOU'LL NEED

Inexpensive clear glass wine goblets
Pencil; scissors
Assorted black, white, and orange patterned scrapbook paper
Halloween stickers
Outdoor decoupage medium, such as Mod Podge
Paintbrush; silver, white, and black waterproof paint markers, optional

HERE'S HOW

1 Trace the base of the wine goblet onto the patterned paper. Cut out the circle. Adhere stickers where desired on the paper circles. Remember that stickers in the center of the circle may be obscured by the stem. Check to see if the desired look is achieved by placing the circle under the base of glass. Make any necessary adjustments.

2 Brush a coat of decoupage medium over the top of the decorated circle. Push the circle onto the base of the wine goblet. Be careful to press out any air that may be trapped in the concave center. Apply another coat of decoupage medium over the underside of paper. Let the glue dry and then follow the package instructions to add three more coats of decoupage medium.

3 To add dimension, use the paint markers to draw spots on the glass over the image if desired. Let the paint dry before use. Carefully hand wash the bowl of the wine goblet and wipe the stem and base clean. The base is water-repellent but will not withstand being submerged in water.

Funky Funnel Candles

Copper coils and metal funnels pair up for a funky Halloween candle display.

WHAT YOU'LL NEED
Newspapers
2 metal funnels with flexible spouts
White spray primer
2 pieces of flexible copper tubing, each 3 to 4 feet long (choose a tubing that fits securely inside the spouts of the funnels)
Acrylic paints in lime green, dark green, magenta, and purple
Flat paintbrush
Flat colored marbles
Strong adhesive, such as E6000
Leaves
Tracing paper; pencil
Scissors
Copper foil
Sharp pencil or pen
Damp cloth
Thin copper wire
Colored gravel
Candles

HERE'S HOW

1 In a well-ventilated work area, cover work surface with newspapers. Spray a light coat of primer onto the inside and outside of metal funnels. Let dry. Spray on a second coat and let dry.

2 Paint a portion of one funnel and flexible tubing piece dark green. Paint the remainder lime green. While still wet, blend the colors together where they meet. Let dry. Paint the second funnel and tubing piece in the same manner using magenta and purple.

3 Glue flat marbles around the outer edges of the funnels.

4 Coil the lengths of tubing into the desired shape, making sure to coil a large enough base to support the funnels upright. Affix one funnel onto end of tubing. If needed, use a little adhesive to secure in place.

5 Trace desired leaves onto tracing paper, cut out, and trace onto copper foil. Cut out foil leaves with care as the edges can be very sharp. Lay copper leaves on a pad of newspapers and trace in vein lines with a sharp pencil or pen, making indentations. Paint the leaves with purple and green acrylic paints. As the paint begins to dry, dab some of it off with a damp cloth, leaving paint in the vein indentations. Let dry.

6 Using copper wire, attach the leaves to the copper tubing. Use a generous length of wire. Coil the ends by wrapping the wire around a pencil and then removing the pencil.

7 Fill the funnels with gravel. Nestle candles in the center of the gravel.

Note: **Never leave a burning candle unattended or in the reach of children.**

Rat Race Snack Set

Serve up a scary snack on these silly dishes. Spiders and rats race toward the center, creating quite a conversation piece for a Halloween party.

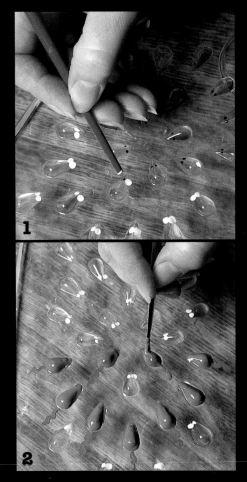

WHAT YOU'LL NEED

Glass snack tray and tumbler (The tray in the photo has raised watermelon seed designs on the bottom. This is a common pattern for snack sets. The tumbler did not come with the set. Pieces like these are often available in flea markets and antique stores.)

Newspapers or waxed paper

Glass paints in white, black, light orange, orange, and purple

Disposable plate; toothpick

Small round paintbrush

Pencil with round eraser

HERE'S HOW

1 Wash and dry the dishes. Avoid touching the areas to be painted.

2 Cover the work surface with newspapers or waxed paper. Turn the tray upside down. Because the painting is done on the bottom of the tray, the painting is done in reverse order. For the eye pupils, dip the end of a toothpick into black paint. Make two dots, approximately ⅛ inch apart, on each pointed end of the watermelon seed designs. Let dry.

3 Dip the handle of a small paintbrush into white paint. Add white dots centered over the black dots as shown in Photo 1, top right. Let dry.

4 Paint the seed shapes either black or gray (a mix of black and white) to make the bodies of spiders and rats as shown in Photo 2. Add eight legs for the spiders and a tail for each rat.

5 Use a toothpick to add three black dots between each rat.

6 For the large dots on the tray and on the glass, dip a pencil eraser into the desired color of paint and dot onto the surface. Let dry. Add smaller dots using the handle end of a paintbrush. Let dry.

7 Paint the tray handle sections alternating black and purple. Let dry.

8 Bake the glassware in the oven if instructed by the paint manufacturer. Let cool. Follow the paint instructions for washing the dishes.

Howls and Owls Candleholder

Flickering like real flames, this layered design casts an eerie illusion.

WHAT YOU'LL NEED

White glass paint; water
Large glass brandy snifter
Paintbrush
Newspapers
Frosted glass spray paint
   in red and yellow
Tracing paper
Pencil
Scissors
Tape
Liquid leading
Small paintbrush

HERE'S HOW

1 Thin white glass paint with water to a drippy consistency. Using the pattern on page 92 as a guide, paint a simple ghost shape on the inside of the glass snifter. Paint random wavy vertical lines as shown in Photo 1, top right. Allow paint to drip and run. Let dry.

2 In a well-ventilated work area, place snifter upside down on newspapers. Spray the rim of snifter with red, fading off several inches from the top edge. Spray the heaviest color toward the rim. Spray the base and stem of snifter. Let dry.

3 Spray over the entire outside with an even coat of yellow as shown in Step 2. Colors will overlap to create a deeper orange and a deep yellow. Let dry.

4 Trace the bat and owl patterns, page 92, or draw any freehand Halloween pattern onto the snifter. Cut out patterns. Tape patterns onto the snifter. Trace around designs. Draw random loops and swirls with a pencil. Remove the patterns.

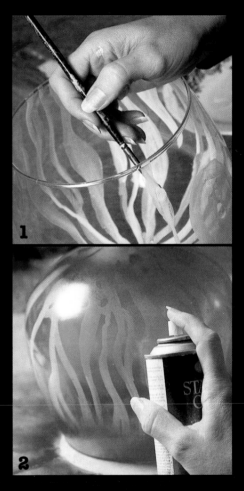

5 Outline the pencil drawing with liquid leading. Use a paintbrush to paint the solid areas. Let dry.

Happy Bones Tumblers

This partying, no-bones-barred clan will get the party off to a swinging start.

WHAT YOU'LL NEED

Tracing paper; pencil
Scissors; clear tape
Glass or plastic tumblers
   with flat sides
Pumpkin
Waterproof paint markers
   in black and white
Acrylic paints in orange,
   purple, green, and black,
   optional
Paintbrushes,
   optional

HERE'S HOW

1 Trace the desired pattern, page 96, and trim ½ inch from design. For the tumblers, tape a pattern inside each glass so the images face out. For the pumpkin, color the back of each pattern with pencil; then tape the patterns to the outside of the pumpkin. Trace the pattern lines on the pumpkin and remove.

2 Use the pattern lines as guides to draw the black skeleton bones and facial features with paint marker. After the black paint has dried, use the white marker to add details. Let the paint dry completely before use. Hand wash the glassware to preserve the images. If desired, paint party hats on the pumpkins.

SKELETON PATTERNS—
TUMBLERS AND PUMPKIN,
PAGES 94-95

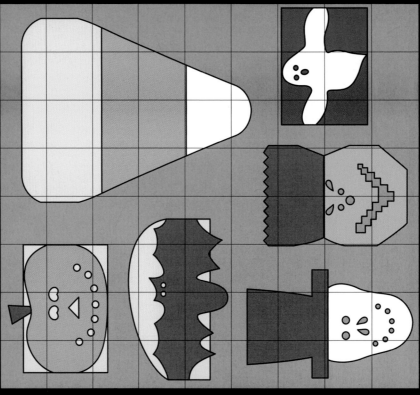

STREAMER PATTERNS   1 SQUARE = 1 INCH

Whether you want to add Halloween accents to shelf and table edges or spruce up the ceiling, the quick-cut paper streamers will do the trick.

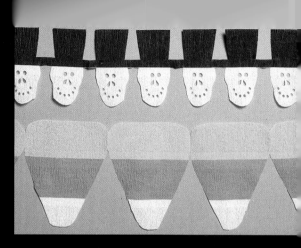

WHAT YOU'LL NEED
Tracing paper; pencil
Crepe paper streamers in white, black, yellow, orange, lime green, and purple
Clear tape; scissors; ruler
Paper punches in round and teardrop shapes
Glue stick

HERE'S HOW

1 Enlarge and trace the desired pattern, opposite. Cut out a rectangle around shape, making sure the sides touch the pattern lines.

2 Measure the width of the pattern rectangle. Working in approximately 2-foot sections, accordion-fold a piece of crepe paper to pattern's width. For the candy, skeleton, and monster, tape the colors together before folding. The bat and the pumpkin are cut out first, then glued to a plain or scalloped piece of yellow crepe paper. The ghost is taped to purple.

3 Trace pattern on one side of folded crepe paper. Cut inside holes using a paper punch. Unfold. Glue cut streamer to a background color if desired. For long streamers, tape them end to end.

get the goodies ready

Only for Halloween could you serve this hair-raising array of drinks, appetizers, and treats. These grossly good recipes will soon be favorites of your little goblins.

Golden Beetle Juice Slush

This tasty concoction is fit for ghouls of all ages.

WHAT YOU'LL NEED

- 1 46-ounce can apricot nectar
- 1 12-ounce can orange juice concentrate, thawed
- 2 16-ounce packages unsweetened sliced peaches, thawed
- 7 12-ounce cans lemon lime carbonated beverage, chilled

HERE'S HOW

1 In a food processor bowl or blender container, add one-third each of the apricot nectar, orange juice concentrate, and sliced peaches. Cover and process or blend until smooth. Pour into a freezer container. Repeat with the remaining nectar, orange juice, and peaches. Cover and seal mixture. Freeze until firm.

2 Scrape about ½ cup of the mixture into each 10-ounce glass. Add an equal amount of carbonated beverage. Stir to combine. Makes 20 servings.

Note: **Wash one-piece plastic toys before adding to slush; remove before drinking.**

Buggy Pasta

This salad may look slimy but it's really delicious!

WHAT YOU'LL NEED

4 ounces fusilli (twisted spaghetti)

4 ounces spaghetti

1 medium yellow squash and/or zucchini, halved lengthwise and sliced

1 cup small cherry tomatoes

1 cup fresh pea pods, tips and strings removed

1 cup pitted ripe olives

1 cup pimiento-stuffed olives

1 cup cubed smoked cheddar cheese or cheddar cheese (4 ounces)

1 cup unblanched whole almonds, toasted

½ cup thinly sliced green onions (4)

1 cup regular or nonfat Italian salad dressing (8 ounces)

HERE'S HOW

1 Cook pasta according to the package directions. Drain the pasta; rinse with cold water and drain again.

2 In a large bowl combine pasta and remaining ingredients except dressing. Add dressing to the pasta mixture; toss gently to coat. Cover and chill 2 to 24 hours. Makes 12 side dish servings.

3 To serve the pasta Halloween-style, place it in a clean plastic cauldron embellished with well-secured plastic spiders.

Finger Foods

These quick-fix finger sandwiches will have everyone biting their nails. Pair them with miniature gravestones for a wonderfully edible duo.

EDIBLE FINGERS

WHAT YOU'LL NEED
Thinly sliced firm-textured
  bread
Chicken salad
Sliced almonds
Cream cheese

HERE'S HOW
1 Remove crust from two slices of bread. Spread some of your favorite chicken salad onto one of the slices. Top with the other slice of bread. Cut lengthwise into ¾-inch-wide strips. With a small knife taper one end of each strip to form a point. Attach a sliced almond to this end with some softened cream cheese, making fingernails.

TOMBSTONE SANDWICHES

WHAT YOU'LL NEED
Hot dog bun
Ham salad
Squeeze bottle mustard
  and catsup

HERE'S HOW
1 Cut a split hot dog bun in half crosswise. Fill the inside of bun with your favorite ham salad. Using squeeze bottle mustard and catsup, mark front of buns with crosses and R.I.P. letters to make tombstones. Stand upright on a serving platter. Makes 2 sandwiches.

Imaginations will soar when partygoers hear the name of this sizzling pizza.

Body Parts Pizza

WHAT YOU'LL NEED

8 ounces skinless, boneless chicken breasts

1 tablespoon cooking oil

1 medium red onion, sliced

1 16-ounce Italian bread shell, such as focaccia

1 cup purchased Alfredo sauce

1 small green sweet pepper, cut into strips

1 tomato, cut into wedges

1 5.3-ounce package cocktail wieners

1 6-ounce jar marinated artichoke hearts, drained

2 tablespoons shredded Parmesan cheese

HERE'S HOW

1 Cut chicken breasts into strips. In a medium skillet heat cooking oil over medium heat. Add chicken and cook about 5 minutes or until chicken strips are golden brown and no longer pink on the inside, turning occasionally. Remove from skillet and set aside. Add onion to skillet, adding additional oil if necessary.

Cook over medium heat about 8 minutes or until onion is tender.

2 Place bread shell on a pizza pan or cookie sheet. Spread Alfredo sauce over shell. Top with chicken strips, onion, green pepper strips, tomato wedges, cocktail wieners, and artichoke hearts. Sprinkle with Parmesan cheese. Bake in a 425° oven for 10 to 15 minutes. Makes 12 to 16 servings.

Spooks on a Stick

Cookies are so much more fun to eat when presented on a stick—especially ones decorated for the bewitching season!

WHAT YOU'LL NEED

Chopped vanilla- and chocolate-flavored candy coating

Orange, green, violet, or yellow paste food coloring

Wood skewers

Crème sandwich cookies

Assorted small candies and nuts

HERE'S HOW

1 Melt small amounts of chopped vanilla- and chocolate-flavored candy coating in separate containers. If desired, add orange, green, violet, or yellow paste food coloring to the vanilla candy coating. Insert a wood skewer into one end of crème sandwich cookie. If cookie begins to open too much, add some melted candy coating to the inside of cookie sandwich, press together around skewer, and chill in refrigerator until firm.

2 Working with one cookie at a time, dip cookie into melted coating, covering completely. Transfer to a cookie sheet lined with waxed paper. While coating is still soft, decorate with small candies and nuts making ghosts, skeletons, witches, pumpkins, monsters, mummies, and owls.

Sticks Mix

Sticks and stones may break your bones but this snack will never hurt you. Use the ingredients listed here or try mixing your own special combination.

WHAT YOU'LL NEED

Pretzel sticks
Sweetened, fruit-flavored
  round toasted cereal
Chocolate-flavored puffed
  corn cereal
Cheese-flavored snacks
Orange and brown
  candy-coated milk
  chocolate pieces

HERE'S HOW

1 Add all ingredients together. Stir gently to mix.

2 Place individual servings in cereal bowls or place mix in one large serving bowl. To serve Halloween-style, place mix in a clean trick-or-treat pail.

Whether you start with a plain purchased layer cake or bake your own, these little creatures are waiting to devour each tasty morsel.

The Rat Cake

WHAT YOU'LL NEED

- 1 2-layer white cake mix
- 3 ounces vanilla-flavored candy coating, chopped
- Violet, orange, green, and yellow food coloring paste
- Small heavy plastic resealable bags
- 2 16-ounce cans vanilla frosting
- Non toxic rubber or plastic mice, rats, snakes, bats, and spiders

HERE'S HOW

1 Prepare cake mix according to package directions. If desired, add orange or green food coloring to batter. Cool.

2 Divide candy coating into three custard cups. Microwave, one at a time, on high for 1 minute or until softened. Stir until melted. Stir in a small amount of violet, orange, or green food coloring into each. Cool slightly. Place each in a resealable bag. Seal and cut the tip from one corner. Make spirals and squiggles on a cookie sheet lined with waxed paper. Chill in refrigerator until set. Keep refrigerated.

3 Tint frosting with yellow and green food coloring for lime green.

4 Wash and dry all animals. Assemble and frost cake. Decorate as desired. Makes 1 cake (12 servings).

Witch Hat Cake

Five layers of round cakes support a pointed ice cream cone to make this towering witch hat.

WHAT YOU'LL NEED

1 package 2-layer white
   cake mix
Green or orange food
   coloring, optional
8-inch wood skewer
1 rolled sugar ice cream cone
2 16-ounce cans chocolate
   fudge frosting
Halloween candies and/or
   large yellow and white
   gumdrops

HERE'S HOW

1 Grease and flour one 9×1½-inch round baking pan and one 9×9×2-inch square baking pan. Prepare cake mix according to package directions, adding green or orange food coloring to batter, if desired. Remove from pans and cool on wire racks. Trim tops of cakes to make even thickness.

2 Cut a 5-, 3½-, and 2½-, and 2-inch circle from the square cake layer. Fill the ice cream cone with cake scraps.

3 Place a small amount of frosting in the middle of a cake plate. Place the 9-inch round cake layer on frosting and press gently to secure.

4 Place about ⅓ cup of the frosting in the center of cake layer and spread to a 5-inch circle. Place the 5-inch circle of cake on top. Spread about ¼ cup frosting in the center of this cake layer and top with the 3½-inch round layer of cake. Spread more frosting and add the 2½- and 2-inch cake layers. Insert an 8-inch wood skewer down through the cake layers for added support. Attach the ice cream cone on top with additional frosting.

5 Frost cake and ice cream cone with remaining frosting (see tip, right). Decorate as desired with candies. Makes 1 cake (12 servings).

Gumdrop Moons and Stars
Use a rolling pin to roll out gumdrops on sugar-coated waxed paper. Cut out moon and star shapes with hors d'oeuvre cutters. Dip cutters in sugar to prevent sticking.

To spread frosting more easily onto sides of cake: Fill a small resealable plastic bag with about 1 cup frosting. Snip off one corner and pipe frosting onto cake sides. Spread evenly.

Constricting Snake Bites

Complete with olive eyes, this slithering fellow is so realistic, you expect him to hiss.

WHAT YOU'LL NEED

3 16-ounce loaves frozen white bread dough, thawed
6 tablespoons brown mustard
16 ounces thinly sliced ham
12 ounces thinly sliced salami
6 ounces provolone cheese, shredded
6 ounces mozzarella cheese, shredded
1 tablespoon water
Green, red, and yellow liquid food coloring
3 egg yolks
2 whole cloves
3 tablespoons grated Parmesan cheese, optional
2 small pimiento-stuffed olives
Bottled roasted red sweet pepper strip (6×1-inch)

HERE'S HOW

1 Line three cookie sheets with foil, grease the foil, and set aside. Roll one of the loaves of dough on a lightly floured surface to a 26×6-inch rectangle. Allow dough to rest a few minutes as needed while rolling. Lightly brush 2 tablespoons mustard to within 1 inch of the sides of dough. Layer one-third of the ham and salami over mustard. Mix together provolone and mozzarella cheeses. Sprinkle one-third of the cheese mixture over ham and salami. Brush edges of dough with water. Roll up into a spiral, starting with one of the long sides. Pinch all edges to seal. Shape dough on baking sheet in an S shape.

2 Combine one of the egg yolks, 1 teaspoon water, and several drops of one food coloring. Repeat to make green, red, and yellow egg wash. Paint stripes crosswise over loaf, allowing the wash to drizzle down sides.

3 Let loaf rise in a warm place for about 20 minutes. Sprinkle top of loaf with 1 tablespoon of the Parmesan cheese if desired.

4 While one section of the snake rises, repeat with remaining bread dough and ingredients. Taper one end of two of these loaves to a rounded point to make a head and tail. Insert 2 whole cloves at one of these ends, making nostrils. Place on prepared cookie sheets. Paint and let rise as above.

5 Bake snake sections in a 375° oven for 25 to 30 minutes or until bottoms of loaves are golden. Insert olives with toothpicks above the cloves to form eyes. Use red pepper strip to make fork tongue. Assemble snake sections on bamboo leaves if desired. Slice and serve warm. Makes 24 slices.

Gutsy Appetizers

Satisfy a snack attack with Spinal Cord Spirals, Fried Gremlin Ears, Spooky Eyeballs, and Oozy Green Pods— if you dare!

SPINAL CORD SPIRALS

WHAT YOU'LL NEED
1 8-ounce package cream cheese, softened
4 8-inch flour tortillas
2 cups spinach leaves or 4 leaf lettuce leaves
2 tomatoes, thinly sliced
6 ounces thinly sliced pepperoni or salami
1 8-ounce package shredded mozzarella cheese (2 cups)

HERE'S HOW
1 Spread 3 tablespoons of the cream cheese to within 1-inch of the edge of a tortilla. Layer with some of the spinach leaves, tomato slices, pepperoni, and ½ cup of the cheese. Tightly roll up into a spiral. Repeat with remaining ingredients.

2 To serve, transfer to a cutting board. Slice off and discard ends. Cut rolls into 1-inch slices. Secure with wooden toothpicks. Stack three or four spirals, slightly off center, to appear as a spinal column. Makes 24.

FRIED GREMLIN EARS

WHAT YOU'LL NEED
1 9-ounce package fresh or frozen cheese-filled tortellini
Green food coloring, optional
1 egg, beaten
¼ cup milk
½ cup Italian-seasoned fine dry bread crumbs

2 tablespoons grated
  Parmesan cheese
Cooking oil
Spaghetti sauce, optional

1 Cook tortellini
according to package
directions. Drain in a
colander, rinse, drain
again, and cool. If desired
fill a large bowl with cold
water. Add several drops of
green food coloring. Add
cooked pasta; let stand 15
to 20 minutes. Drain well.
Combine egg and milk in a
large bowl. Add tortellini
and toss gently to coat.
Combine bread crumbs and
Parmesan cheese in a plastic
bag. Lift tortellini with a
slotted spoon and add
about one-fourth at a time
to crumb mixture. Toss to
coat with crumbs. Remove.

2 Add about 12 tortellini
to deep, hot oil (365°).
Fry for 1 minute or until
golden brown. Remove
with a slotted spoon and
drain on paper towels.
Transfer to a cookie sheet
and keep warm in a 300°
oven while frying
remaining tortellini. Serve

warm with spaghetti sauce
if desired. Makes 78 ears.

SPOOKY EYEBALLS

WHAT YOU'LL NEED
1 1½-pound spaghetti
  squash
3 tablespoons bottled
  ranch salad dressing
24 large cherry tomatoes
24 pimiento-stuffed olives

HERE'S HOW

1 Cut squash in half
lengthwise; remove
seeds. Place squash halves
cut side down in a baking
dish. Bake in a 350° oven
for 30 to 40 minutes or
until tender. Or place
halves cut side down in
a microwave-safe baking
dish with ¼ cup water.
Microwave, covered, on
high 17 minutes or until
tender, turning once.

2 Using a fork, scrape
squash to make into
long shreds. You should
have about 2 cups cooked
squash. Place squash in
a bowl; stir in salad
dressing. Cut off tops of
cherry tomatoes. Use a

small spoon to hollow out
tomatoes. Fill centers with
cooked spaghetti squash.
Place a pimiento-stuffed
olive in the center of the
squash mixture in each
tomato. Cover and chill up
to 4 hours before serving.
Makes 24 servings.

OOZY GREEN PODS

WHAT YOU'LL NEED
24 pea pods
1 8-ounce tub cream cheese
  with garlic and herbs
2 tablespoons finely
  chopped carrot
2 tablespoons finely
  chopped red sweet pepper
2 tablespoons finely chopped
  green sweet pepper

HERE'S HOW

1 Remove tips and strings
from pea pods. Cut open
one long side of each pea
pod. Set aside. In a small
bowl stir together remaining
ingredients. Place mixture
in a small resealable
plastic bag. Close bag. Cut
off one corner from bag and
squeeze mixture into
opened pods. Makes 24.

Bat Wings

Tell the kids they're eating bat wings and they are sure to request them even when it's not Halloween!

WHAT YOU'LL NEED

20 chicken wings
  (3½ pounds)
½ cup soy sauce
2 teaspoons grated fresh
  ginger or ½ teaspoon
  ground ginger
¼ teaspoon crushed red
  pepper
1 teaspoon five spice
  powder
2 cloves garlic, minced
1 recipe Swamp Dip

HERE'S HOW

1 Place wings in a plastic bag set in a shallow dish. In a small bowl stir together soy sauce, ginger, crushed red pepper, five spice powder and garlic. Pour over wings. Close bag and toss to coat. Chill in refrigerator several hours or overnight, turning bag occasionally. Remove wings from bag, reserving the marinade.

2 Place wings on a 15×10×1-inch baking pan lined with foil. Bake, uncovered, in a 450° oven for 10 minutes. Brush with reserved marinade (discard remaining marinade). Bake 15 to 20 minutes longer or until chicken is tender and no longer pink. Serve with Swamp Dip. Makes 20 appetizers.

Swamp Dip:
In a small bowl stir together an 8-ounce container of dairy sour cream and 3 tablespoons coarse ground mustard. Garnish with fresh whole chives. Serve with bat wings.

TO MAKE THE PUMPKIN

1 Cut off the top of a pumpkin. Scoop out the insides.

2 Press a bat cookie cutter randomly into the pumpkin, making an impression through the pumpkin skin. Use a sharp paring knife to carve the bat shapes. Insert a candle, replace the lid, and light the candle through one of the openings.

Note: **Never leave a burning candle unattended or in the reach of children.**

get all dressed up

Whether you want to impress someone or freak them out, these disguises and jewelry accents are just what Dr. Frankenstein ordered. Go ahead and wrap your wrists in bugs and bones or become a witch—just for a day.

Bug Jewelry

These slimy sensations will let everyone know that you're in the mood for Halloween tricks. Made from fishing bait, you can create a stringer full of crazy combinations.

WHAT YOU'LL NEED
24-gauge wire; wire cutter
T and O ring and/or
    jump ring clasps
Glass beads
Seed beads

Assorted rubber
    bait, including
    spinner bait
    trailers, lilifiddler
    legs, and frogs
Waxed paper

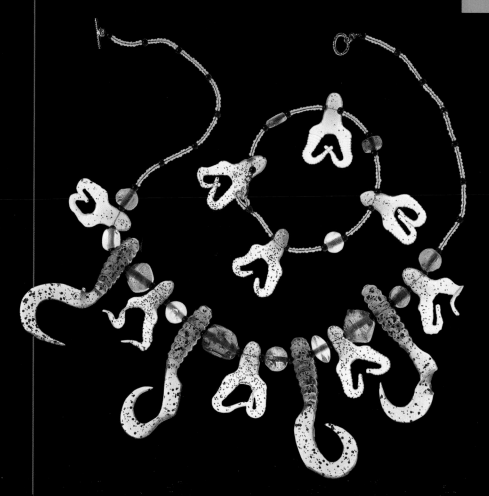

HERE'S HOW
1 Cut desired length of wire to make a bracelet or necklace. Hook a clasp onto one end of the wire.
2 Thread beads onto the open end of the wire. To add bait, push the wire end through the thickest portion of the rubber. Continue by alternating desired beads with bait. Hook the other end of the clasp to the wire end.
3 To store, place between waxed paper sheets.

Fancy Flapper

Dance your way back to the 1920s with this flashy little number.

WHAT YOU'LL NEED
2 tab-top curtain panels in desired color with decorative bottom
Scissors; thread; needle
Elastic sequin trim
Feathers
Purchased boa, long gloves, jewelry, and fishnet stockings

HERE'S HOW

1 Cut off the tabs from the curtain tops. Fold one piece in half lengthwise. Allowing for desired width, cut out rounded underarm shapes. Repeat for dress back.

2 Stitch side seam leaving a slit at the bottom edge. Stitch elastic sequin trim around armholes and along the front and the back of the bodice, stretching the trim as it is stitched.

3 For the headband, stitch a length of elastic sequin trim into the desired size loop. Stitch feathers to sequin trim.

4 Accessorize costume with a purchased boa, long gloves, jewelry, and fishnet stockings.

fold

DRESS DIAGRAM

118

This wand-waving wizard will want to wear the sparkling costume even after Halloween—for performing magic shows and playing make-believe.

Willy Wizard

WHAT YOU'LL NEED
Tape measure; pencil
1 yard of star fabric or
   shower curtain; thread
Fusible interfacing; ribbon
Pinking shears; star stamp
Silver glitter fabric paint
Metallic silver rickrack
½-inch diameter dowel; saw
Acrylic paint in royal blue
   and silver glitter; button
Paintbrush; purchased hat,
   shirt, pants, and gloves

HERE'S HOW

1 For cape, measure from back of neck downward to determine length. Fold star fabric in half so center back of cape is on fold (see cape diagram, page 131). Draw a curve to make a quarter circle. Cut out a neckline.

2 Fuse a 2-inch-wide strip of interfacing around neck edge. Trim neck and bottom edges of cape with pinking shears. Fringe the bottom edge with straight scissors.

3 Make ½-inch slits approximately 1 inch apart in neck facing. Thread ribbon through slits, ending with ribbon on the right side. Gather slightly. Sew a button on ribbon through cape to secure gathers.

4 Stamp stars with silver glitter fabric paint. Stitch two rows of metallic rickrack around cape edge.

5 For wand, cut an 18-inch length of dowel. Paint royal blue; let dry. Paint with silver glitter paint. While wet, wrap with rickrack; let dry. Add one more coat of silver glitter over rickrack. Let dry.

Little Red Riding Hood

With a basket for goody getting, this little costume will win oodles of smiles.

WHAT YOU'LL NEED

Measuring tape; scissors
Red plaid round tablecloth
Fusible hem tape; elastic
3 yards pre-gathered lace
Red fabric or flat sheet
Ruffled red trim; red ribbon
Red sport weight yarn
¼ yard pre-gathered lace
White blouse and basket

HERE'S HOW

1 For skirt, measure waist. Make a circle pattern the same circumference as the waist measurement. Cut out circle from center of tablecloth. Trim tablecloth if necessary to shorten.

2 Use fusible hem tape to press under 1 inch of raw edge at waist, clipping as necessary. Make small slits in waistline hem about 1½ inches apart. Thread elastic through the slits; adjust to fit waist. Sew lace around bottom hem.

3 For cape, measure from back of neck downward to determine length. Fold fabric in half so center back of cape is on fold. Draw a curve to make a quarter circle. Cut out a rounded neckline. Use diagram, left, to draw hood portion of cape. Cut out.

4 Stitch lace at edge of hood. With yarn, make a gathering stitch at bottom of hood where indicated on diagram; secure at sides. Work gathering stitch along hood edge. Add ribbon ties.

fold

gathering line for hood

HOODED CAPE DIAGRAM

Bootiful Bat

No one will fear this nocturnal nymph that has a wingspan larger than any bat around.

WHAT YOU'LL NEED

60×60-inch piece of black fabric
White sewing pencil
Scissors
Fusible facing
Elastic
Sequin trim in silver and red
Thread
Black buttons
Purchased black sweatshirt, black leggings or sweatpants, bat ears, and white gloves; plastic fangs

HERE'S HOW

1 Fold the fabric in half to form a triangle. Using the photograph for inspiration, draw lines for the wings.

2 Cut out the wings through both layers using the diagram, right, for inspiration. Cut out a center circle for the neck. Adjust size of cape at the arms and head opening according to the child.

3 Fuse facing inside the neck opening. Make small slits in neck facing about 1½ inches apart. Thread elastic through the slits; adjust to fit.

4 For trim, stitch a single row of silver sequin trim along each line in the wing front and back. Stitch red sequin trim around the bottom edge.

5 Fit cape wings on the child. Sew two sets of black buttons at the underarm through both layers to secure the cape on the arms.

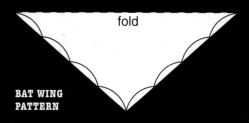

fold

BAT WING PATTERN

Bone Bangles

Before you head out to your next ghostly gala, put on this rattling set of skeleton bones. Wear them around your neck and your wrist—they're the perfect costume jewelry for every costume party!

WHAT YOU'LL NEED

Pearl white polymer clay, such as Premo Sculpey or Granitex
Silver eye pins
Silver jump rings
Needlenose pliers
Small wire cutters
Silver T and O clasps

HERE'S HOW

1 Mold ½- to ¾-inch bones out of polymer clay. Insert an eye pin into either end of each bone so that only the circular eyes extend beyond the end of the bone. You will need to trim many of the eye pins with wire cutters before inserting them into the bones.

2 Bake the bones according to the clay manufacturer's instructions.

3 To join the bones, use needlenose pliers to make a small gap in the jump ring. Hook two bone ends onto the ring and then carefully use the pliers to close the jump ring. Continue working in this fashion until you've linked together enough bones to make a bracelet or necklace. Attach an extra jump ring on either end of the bone chain to connect both the T clasp and the O ring.

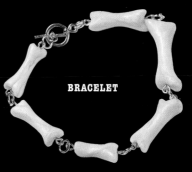

NECKLACE

BRACELET

123

BLACK AND ORANGE HAT

WHAT YOU'LL NEED
Tracing paper
Pencil
Scissors
Heavy orange paper
Black paper
Black glitter paint
Orange fabric paint
Thick white crafts glue
Double-stick tape
Black pipe cleaners
Orange beads

HERE'S HOW

1 Enlarge and trace the hat pattern on page 127, cut out, and transfer onto orange and black papers as shown in photo. Cut out.

2 Use black glitter paint to draw random coil shapes on the orange paper. Let dry. Paint orange wavy lines down the center of the black strips.

3 Place a piece of double-stick tape down one edge of orange paper and shape the paper into a cone.

4 Use a dab of glue to affix the black strips to the top and bottom of hat. Fold a small tip of the narrow end and insert into the tip of cone.

5 Put assorted orange beads onto ends of pipe cleaners and insert into the tip of the hat with a small dab of glue.

EYEBALL HAT

WHAT YOU'LL NEED
Tracing paper
Pencil
Scissors
Heavy green paper
Purple stretch fleece fabric
Double-stick tape
Green felt
Spray adhesive
Plastic eyeballs
Two 1½-inch plastic foam balls, such as Styrofoam
Orange acrylic paint
Paintbrush
Thick white crafts glue
Pipe cleaner

instructions continued on page 126

Put on any of these
Halloween hats and you'll
be ready to party until
the bats come home!

HERE'S HOW

1 Enlarge and trace the hat pattern (without the spiderweb design), opposite, and draw a 4-inch-long triangle onto tracing paper, cut out, and trace onto green paper and purple fabric. Cut out fabric and paper. Cut out about six green triangles.

2 Shape the paper into a cope and secure with double-stick tape.

3 Spray a coat of adhesive to the outside of the green paper hat.

4 Attach the eyeballs randomly in pairs.

5 Wrap the purple fabric around the hat, aligning the shape and covering the eyeballs. The fleece will stick to the adhesive on the paper. Add a strip of double-stick tape at the seam if needed.

6 Feeling the eyeballs through the fabric, cut small horizontal slits in the fabric over the eyeballs.

7 Paint the foam balls with acrylic paint. Let dry. Glue on eyeballs with crafts glue. Let dry.

8 Bend a pipe cleaner in half and insert a foam ball on each end. Insert and glue folded end of pipe cleaner into tip of hat.

9 Glue triangles onto the bottom edge of hat, overlapping each other.

SPIDER HAT

WHAT YOU'LL NEED
Tracing paper
Pencil
Scissors
Heavy black paper
Utility knife
White paint pen
Double-stick tape
8 orange wavy
   pipe cleaners
Thick white crafts glue
2-inch foam ball, such
   as Styrofoam
Orange acrylic paint
Paintbrush
2 plastic eyes
Orange ribbon

HERE'S HOW

1 Trace hat pattern, opposite, onto tracing paper, cut out, and trace onto black paper. Cut out black hat shape.

2 Use a utility knife to very lightly score along score lines as shown on pattern. Draw in web lines using a white paint pen. Let dry.

3 Run a piece of double-stick tape along one edge of hat, coil into a cone, and affix ends together.

4 Twist eight orange wavy pipe cleaners together at one end and insert that end into the tip of the hat. Add a dab of glue for extra support. Bend pipe cleaners into spider legs.

5 Paint foam ball orange and let dry. Glue onto top center of hat. Glue eyeballs onto foam ball.

6 Make hat ties using orange ribbon.

SPIDER HAT PATTERN

1 SQUARE = 1 INCH

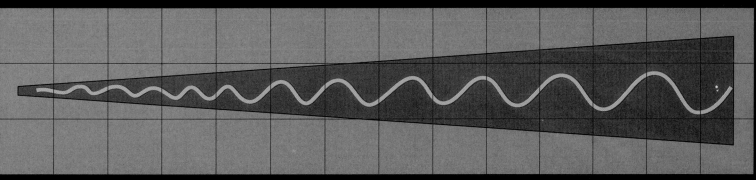

BLACK AND ORANGE HAT PATTERN

1 SQUARE = 1 INCH

Whoa Nelly Nurse

You'll be surprised how disguised you'll be behind long golden locks, flashy eyeglasses, and bright red lipstick.

WHAT YOU'LL NEED

Measuring tape
Round white tablecloth
Scissors; needle
Fusible hem tape; elastic
Thread in red and white
60-inch square piece of
   white fabric; interfacing
Pinking shears
Red sequin trim; ribbon
2 pieces of 6-inch square
   red fabric; button
Purchased wig, hat,
   hot water bottle,
   stethoscope,
   white hose and
   shoes

HERE'S HOW

1 For skirt, measure waist. Make a circle pattern the circumference of the waist measurement. Cut this circle from tablecloth center (diagram, page 131).

2 Use fusible hem tape to press under 1 inch of raw edge at waist, clipping as necessary. Make small slits in waistline hem about 1½ inches apart. Thread elastic through the slits; adjust to fit waist.

3 For cape, measure from back of neck downward to determine length. Fold white fabric in half so center back of cape is on fold. Draw a curve to make a quarter circle (diagram, page 131). Cut out a rounded neckline.

4 Fuse a 2-inch-wide piece of interfacing around neck edge. Hem center front along selvage. Pink lower edge. Stitch red sequin trim close to outer edge. To make red crosses, cut out 2-inch squares from each corner of red fabric pieces. Fuse crosses at lower front corners of cape.

5 Make ½-inch slits approximately 1 inch apart in neck facing. Thread ribbon through slits, ending with ribbon on the right side. Gather slightly. Sew a button on ribbon through cape to secure gathers.

Bring back a little piece of history with this comfy costume for gals of any age.

Betsy Ross

WHAT YOU'LL NEED
60×89 blue-check oval
   tablecloth
Scissors
Thread
Needle
Fusible tape
Elastic
20-inch-diameter circle of
   light blue fabric
45×45-inch piece of red
   calico or purchased
   afghan; pre-gathered lace
Purchased blouse, sewing
   basket, embroidery hoop,
   and star fabric

HERE'S HOW

1 For the skirt, cut the tablecloth lengthwise, allowing for the desired length plus 1 inch (diagram, below). Overlap skirt at front for closure and baste along top edge.

2 Use fusible tape to fuse under 1 inch of raw edge along the top edge of the waist. Cut slits every 2 inches and thread elastic through slits. Adjust to fit waist and tie ends.

3 For bonnet, stitch pre-gathered lace around outside edge of light blue fabric circle. Stitch elastic 2 inches in from outer edge.

4 For the shawl, use red calico fabric or a purchased afghan.

cutting line

SKIRT DIAGRAM

129

Hazel and Broomhilda

After parking their brooms at the door, these witty witches are ready for some party brew. With such easy-to-make skirts and capes, you can transform into a witch in the blink of a cat's eye.

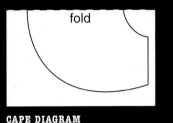

CAPE DIAGRAM

SKIRT DIAGRAM

WHAT YOU'LL NEED

Tape measure
Pencil; scissors
70-inch round tablecloth
   for adult skirt
60-inch round tablecloth
   for youth skirt
Fusible hem tape
1 yard of black fabric or
   round tablecloth*
Pinking shears
Elastic; ribbon
Interfacing; button
Purchased shirts and hats

HERE'S HOW

1 For each skirt, measure the waist of the person that will be wearing the costume. Make a circle pattern the same circumference as the waist measurement. Cut out this circle from the tablecloth center.

2 Use fusible hem tape to press under 1 inch of raw edge at waist, clipping as necessary to make pressing easy. Make small slits in waistline hem about 1½ inches apart. Thread elastic through the slits; adjust to fit waist.

3 For cape, measure from back of neck downward to determine length. Fold fabric in half so center back of cape is on fold. Draw a curve to make a quarter circle. Cut out a rounded neckline. If using a tablecloth to make capes, simply cut in half and cut out rounded necklines.

4 Fuse interfacing or fabric around neck edge about 2 inches wide. Trim neck and bottom edges with pinking shears. Fringe the bottom edge with straight scissors.

5 Make ½-inch slits approximately 1 inch apart in neck facing. Thread ribbon through slits, ending with ribbon on the right side. Gather slightly. Sew a button on ribbon through cape to secure gathers. Don purchased hats and shirts.

*Note: Look in the linen department for tablecloths, flat panel curtain sheets, and shower curtains. When making cape, cut with front edge on hem by folding panel crosswise. Shower curtains and sheets provide wide widths of fabric with no seams. Round tablecloths make one skirt or two capes.

treat
them right

When costumed cuties come to call, surprise
them with Halloween treats packaged festively
in hand-decorated pails, pumpkins, bags, and
boxes. They'll love you to death for it!

Checkerboard Bags

Treat your partygoers with a sack that's big enough to hold oodles of Halloween surprises. Woven crepe paper streamers create a vivid checkerboard that camouflages the lunch sack underneath.

WHAT YOU'LL NEED

Paper lunch sack
Ruler
Pencil
Crepe paper streamers in 2 Halloween colors
Scissors
Stapler
Glue stick

HERE'S HOW

1 From the bottom of bag, measure up 7 inches. Make a mark. Fold the top of the bag to the inside along the mark.

2 Cut eight lengths of one color streamer, each 11 inches long. Cut four lengths of the remaining color streamer, each 18 inches long.

3 For each of the short vertical streamers, overlap 1 inch of streamer inside the top of the bag. Staple in place. Fold the streamers over the bag top, bringing to the outside.

4 For the long horizontal streamers, glue the streamer ends to one side, alternating over and under the vertical streamer. Beginning with the top streamer, weave each one over and under the vertical streamers. Secure the ends with glue.

5 Glue the ends of the vertical streamers to the bottom of the sack. Let dry.

Bewitching Treat Holder

With a party hat base, this happy witch is the topper for a round goody box.

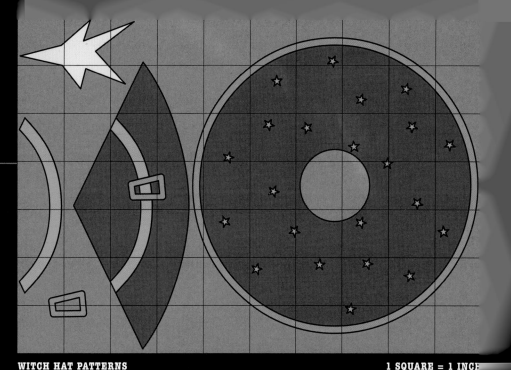

WITCH FACE FULL-SIZE PATTERNS

WITCH HAT PATTERNS

WHAT YOU'LL NEED

Small party hat

Staple remover

Crafting foam in lime
green, light pink, dark
pink, white, black,
purple, and yellow

Pencil; scissors; stapler

Tracing paper

Pinking shears; paper punch

Glue for foam and plastic

Awl; 6 black pipe cleaners

Star paper punch

12-inch-long piece of
1½-inch-wide black
grosgrain ribbon

Round papier-mâché box

HERE'S HOW

1 Remove staples from
party hat. Lay hat flat
on lime green foam. Trace
the shape. Using the hat
again as a pattern, trace
around the top 2 inches of
the hat point on black foam.
Connect the sides with a
U-shape scallop. Cut out the
green and black pieces. Align
the black foam over the tip
of the green hat shape and
staple where ends join.
Staple the party hat back
together. Place the green
foam over the hat shape and
staple at the seam to secure.

2 Enlarge and/or trace the
patterns, above. Cut out
the shapes. Trace around the
pattern pieces on the
appropriate color of
crafting foam. Cut out the
shapes using scissors or
pinking shears as desired.

3 Glue the face pieces in
place. Punch a hole

from foam for the wart
on the nose. Glue in place.
Let the glue dry.

4 Cut the pipe cleaners
in half. Wrap around a
medium-size marking pen
and remove. Use an awl to
poke holes in the top of the
green cone, three on each
side. Glue one end of each
pipe cleaner inside a hole.
Let dry.

5 Pull the foam brim over
the hat point. Glue on
the hatband, buckle, and
star. Punch approximately
30 stars from yellow foam.
Glue on hat brim and in
hair. Let dry.

6 Glue ribbon around
papier-mâché box
bottom. Let dry.

Terrifying Trio

Papier-mâché boxes are just the right size to hold a handful of treats. This trio of characters uses bell, oval, and tree shapes.

WHAT YOU'LL NEED
Acrylic paints in black, white, dark lime green, purple, and orange
Paintbrush; fan paintbrush
Purchased papier-mâché boxes in bell, oval, and tree shapes
Crackle medium
Tracing paper; pencil
Transfer paper
Pencil with round-tip eraser; round toothpick

HERE'S HOW

1 For the skeleton, base-coat the bottom of the box with white and the lid with black as in Photo 1. Let dry. Apply a second coat and let dry.

2 Paint a thick coat of crackle medium over the painted areas. Let dry. To achieve the crackled look, paint black over the white, trying not to overlap strokes. Paint the black lid using white as shown in Photo 2. Let dry.

3 For all boxes, trace the desired pattern on page 138. Place transfer paper between pattern and box lid and retrace the pattern lines to transfer the design. Remove pattern and transfer paper.

4 Paint in the background areas, using the patterns as guides. Let the paint dry. Paint in the details. For large dots, such as the witch's eyes, dip the eraser end of a pencil into paint and dot onto the surface. For small dots, dip a toothpick into paint and dot onto surface. If layering dots or other motifs, let paint dry between coats.

5 For the edge of the skeleton and the hair on the witch and dracula, use a fan brush. Using very little paint, make short strokes from the outer edge inward as shown in Photo 3. Repeat until the desired look is achieved. Let dry.

1

2

3

TERRIFYING TRIO PATTERNS

138

Floral Cones

Sequin hearts are arranged as dainty flowers on this pretty see-through treat cone.

WHAT YOU'LL NEED

Purchased acrylic cone (available at crafts stores)
Heart-shape sequins in orange and purple
Thick white crafts glue
Gold beads
Paper punch
1 pink and 1 yellow pipe cleaner

HERE'S HOW

1 Arrange five of the same color of sequins in a circle to form a flower shape. Glue in place. Glue orange and purple heart flowers randomly on the cone. Let dry.

2 Glue a gold bead in the center of each flower. Let the glue dry.

3 Punch a hole ½ inch from top of cone. Punch a second hole opposite the first. Twist two pipe cleaners together. Thread the pipe cleaners through the holes, securing to the cone by twisting the pipe cleaner ends upward. Shape the pipe cleaners into a handle.

Bat Treat Bags

Ready to take flight
with a bag of
goodies, this treat
bat has a fuzzy
body and head.

WHAT YOU'LL NEED
Tracing paper
Pencil
Scissors
Black paper
Fall colored papers
Black crafting foam
Black marker
Thick white crafts glue
Green paper treat bag
Purple fuzzy balls
Plastic eyeballs
2 black pipe cleaners

HERE'S HOW

1 Enlarge and trace patterns, left, onto tracing paper. Cut out and trace onto black and colored papers. Cut out leaves and bat wings. Cut ears from fun foam or paper.

2 Outline leaves and leaf veins with black marker. Glue leaves randomly on the bag.

3 Fan-fold bat wings as shown in photo above right. Glue purple balls onto center of wings. Glue on eyes and ears. Poke holes in wings and insert black pipe cleaners to form legs.

LEAF PATTERNS · 1 SQUARE = 1 INCH

BAT WING PATTERN · 1 SQUARE = 1 INCH

Metal pails come in a variety of sizes for sharing candy or other Halloween surprises. Add a coat of paint, a sticker, and glitter for a magical touch.

Painted Pails

WHAT YOU'LL NEED
Newspapers
Metal pail
Matte black spray paint
Halloween stickers
Paintable glitter
Paintbrush
Shredded paper or Mylar
Halloween candy
Curling ribbon; scissors

HERE'S HOW

1 In a well-ventilated work area, cover work surface with newspapers. Place pail on newspapers. Lift the handle up. Spray-paint the interior of the pail. Paint the pail sides and handle. Let the paint dry. Apply a second coat of paint. Let dry.

2 Apply a Halloween sticker to one side of the pail. Smooth onto surface by gently rubbing with your finger.

3 Paint glitter over the handle. Paint glitter over the sticker, extending the glitter around the sticker in an irregular shape. Let the glitter dry.

4 Fill the pail with shredded paper or Mylar. Add candies to fill the pail.

5 Tie curling ribbon around the handle. Curl by pulling the ribbon tightly against scissors blade. Trim the ribbon ends if desired.

Etched Jars

Start collecting glass jars to make these strikingly sturdy containers for Halloween sweets and snacks.

WHAT YOU'LL NEED
Glass jar
Etching cream
Paintbrush
Rubber gloves
Colored paper in orange, purple, lime green, white, or yellow
Dish soap
Ruler; scissors; tape
Pipe cleaners in white, black, orange, yellow, purple, lime green, metallic gold, or metallic silver

HERE'S HOW

1 Paint the exterior of the jar with etching cream as shown in Photo 1. Apply a thick, even coat. Etch the jar according to the manufacturer's directions.

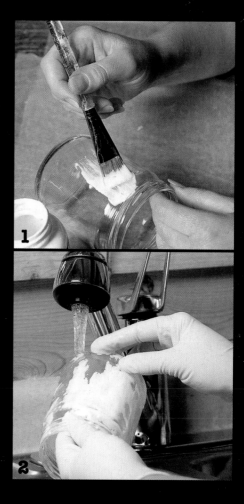

2 Put on rubber gloves. Rinse etching cream off thoroughly in sink , as in Photo 2. Rinse sink well. Wash jar with dish soap. Let dry.

3 Using a computer, type MONSTER MIX, BOO, TRICK-OR-TREAT, or other Halloween words or phrases. Enlarge the type so it will fill the desired space, vertically or horizontally, on the jar. Print the word(s) on colored paper.

4 Measure the height of the jar and trim the paper to that size. Roll the paper strip and insert into the jar. If needed, trim the paper ends so they do not overlap onto the lettering. From the inside of the jar, tape the paper so that the roll maintains its shape.

5 Braid, twist, or wrap pipe cleaners to trim rim of jar. Wrap pipe cleaners around jar and twist the ends to secure.

Index

Designers

Photography

Photo Styling—Carol Dahlstrom
Photo Styling Assistant—
    Donna Chesnut
Food Styling—Diana Nolin